PEOPLE SPACE

Norman Ashcraft: B.A. University of California, Berkeley
                   Ph.D. Brandeis University

Anthropologist and writer who has studied the problems of poverty and of the family in Latin America, the Caribbean, Europe, and New York City. His previous publications include a monograph citing the problems of poverty in one small underdeveloped country, a number of articles on poverty and the family, the family in America, and growing up in America, and he has edited two books on the American family and education in underdeveloped countries. He recently collaborated with Albert Scheflen on a textbook on the theory of human territoriality. He presently lives in Manhattan and teaches anthropology at Adelphi University.

Albert E. Scheflen: Sc.B. Dickinson College, Carlisle,
                      Pennsylvania
                      M.D. University of Pennsylvania,
                      Philadelphia, Pa.

Psychiatrist, communication theorist, and urbanologist who has studied small group behavior, the American family, and urban territoriality. His previous works include many papers on psychiatry, psychoanalysis, and human communication, three books on communication, and one on the nature of human territories. He presently lives in the Bronx and teaches at the Bronx Psychiatric Center and the Albert Einstein College of Medicine.

PEOPLE SPACE

The Making and Breaking of Human Boundaries

Norman Ashcraft
and
Albert E. Scheflen

ANCHOR BOOKS
ANCHOR PRESS/DOUBLEDAY
GARDEN CITY, NEW YORK
1976

Anchor Books Edition: 1976

Library of Congress Cataloging in Publication Data

Ashcraft, Norman.
People space.

Bibliography: p. 176
Includes index.
1. Personal space. 2. Social interaction.
3. Nonverbal communication. 4. Space (Architecture)
I. Scheflen, Albert E., joint author. II. Title.
HM291.A84   301.11
Library of Congress Catalog Card Number 76–2844
ISBN: 0-385-11229-7

TO MARGARET MEAD

Dr. Mead has been at the forefront of almost every innovation in the study of man for over forty years, and no one else has been more important in conveying these ideas to the people. She has been a pioneer in the audiovisual techniques and methods of research that underlie this work.

PREFACE

In early 1970 Norman Ashcraft and Albert Scheflen met at the Bronx Psychiatric Center in New York. Ashcraft, an anthropologist who had studied the family and problems of poverty in the Caribbean and Western Europe, was learning more about poverty and family life styles in America. Scheflen, a psychiatrist who had been a pioneer in the family therapy movement and communication theory, especially "body language" had put together a research project to examine the problems of urban territorial disruption in ghetto communities. It was a mutually beneficial meeting, for it set in motion six years of research and collegial association.[1]

The present collaboration is not just another effort to summarize research findings, as important as that may be. The authors believe that there is a larger problem to be explored: what kinds of things will be considered important when we try to comprehend human affairs and how will they be explained?[2]

This book is about how people use space in various contexts, how this use is repeated and replicated at various points of interaction, whether in an open public space or in the confines of one's home, and how this use is repeated and replicated from the level of typical conversational settings to the layouts of rooms, houses, neighborhoods, and cities.

Our perspective is territorial, for we want to describe what people actually do with the spaces they have and use, how they live, and how they attempt to make do. Within this framework, we intend to look at a variety of human problems —poverty, scarcity of resources, ethnic differences, violence, crowding, privacy—not as they have evolved from the genes of man but as they have evolved from the behaviors of man. We should be prepared now to see the richness of human activities for what they are: a product of all those behaviors past, present, and future that in combination make up the activities of a single event.

ACKNOWLEDGMENTS

Much of the material appearing in this book is based on the findings of a five-year study of the problems of urban territoriality. We owe an intellectual debt to those scholars who broke ground in the general study of territoriality: Hall, Watson, Lorenz, Wynne-Edwards, Tinbergen, and Sommer. Scheflen is especially indebted to Ray L. Birdwhistell, I. Charles Kaufman, and Glen McBride, who helped him understand territoriality and its problems.

A number of members of the research project directly contributed to the findings described here: Adam Kendon, Robert McMillan, Clarence Robins, Joseph Schaeffer, Ronald Goodrich, Charlene Thacker, Mary Powers, and especially Kenneth Gospodinoff, who labored with us in this effort. We are greatly indebted to Mrs. Yetta Sherman, who helped get the manuscript out and supervised the typists, Jeanne Bouza and Barbara Mitnick.

The research was supported by the VanAmeringen Foundation, by the Center for Metropolitan Studies of the National Institutes of Mental Health, Grants ℀5R01-MH15977 and 7R01-MH18162, and by the Bronx Psychiatric Center and the Albert Einstein College of Medicine. The authors are solely responsible for the remarks that appear in this book.

CONTENTS

Part I
USING SPACE

Chapter 1
TERRITORIES

Man is a territorial animal very much like his fellow creatures. He defines a space and marks it out for his particular use. He draws visible and invisible boundaries which he expects others to respect. He will defend a territory against the intrusions of others.

Each nation-state attempts to reinforce its integrity with physical borders that are fixed and recognized. The traveler soon learns that he has encountered a border as immigration authorities and customs officials descend to mark his entry and frequently his exit. Even in those areas of undisputed borders and friendly relations the ritual continues. Canadians and United States citizens cross one another's boundaries by the hundreds of thousands and their governments ease the transition with only the most perfunctory statement of form and national identity. At the borders of southern Germany and Austria, thousands of Germans rush to the Austrian mountains on weekends. The border guards hardly take notice as the passports flash in their faces and the automobiles speed on to pleasure and sightseeing. Tourists regard the border crossing as a nuisance, but the ritual serves to mark territorial recognition. And if the border passing is not enough, the change of currency adds to the distinction.

We buy a piece of property and, in the process of exchange, the state demands a survey. Once produced, the survey fixes the legal borders. We can then plant hedges, gardens, build fences, or even mow our lawns in a different direction. We repaint, rewallpaper, possibly even alter the structure slightly. We bring in our furniture and then open the wine and by candlelight toast our "new property." It is finally ours.

Inside the home there may be definite territories. This chair is Dad's and that is that! We may raid the refrigerator, but don't rearrange the kitchen or there will be trouble with Mom. Other areas or objects in the home may be more or less ambiguous. A toothbrush is rarely a disputed territory. But a towel will gain its description from the conventions of the household. Dishes and utensils, with those obvious exceptions of the personalized coffee mug, etc., are less likely to be an item of personal territory. The house may be family communal property, its decoration being worked out through negotiation or fiat. But even within the sanctity of home, there may be disputes over personal versus public territory. Parents, for instance, may not recognize as private a drawer in their teen-age daughter's bedroom. Yet should the girl go through her mother's purse, the parents might lecture her about privacy.

When we use the word "territory," most of us think of a definable or definite area of land, a tract of space. And in one sense of the term this is accurate, for many have referred to territorial behavior as just that—a concrete representation of space. A territory can be the immediate area surrounding a water hole. It can be a nation, a county, a community, the family yard.

But behaviors and styles of living can be as different as the nations which issue different passports. Americans who think they are in the same English-speaking territory may abruptly encounter Canadian nationalism. Germans and Austrians supposedly speak the same language, and Bavarians speak almost the same dialect as their Tirolean neighbors. But there are culturally distinctive markers which even the most casual observer soon notices. We are all familiar with the regional differences within the territory of the United States. The New Englander is as distinct in life style from his Texan counterpart as are their separate dialects. Italian-Americans share with Irish-Americans not only those attitudes that have made them American but their religious beliefs as well. But few of us would have any trouble recognizing the differences in behavior that mark their ethnic traditions. Territories are more than just physical things, hunks of space.[1]

While both man and animals bound space, in no system is this space absolute. It only takes on the appearance of absoluteness given the behaviors of animals. Walls and fences are visible and appear to be fixed. But even such an object as the Great Wall of China, which is in fact several walls, becomes an important indicator of Chinese history when examined through a concept of "wallness." As a physical object, the Great Wall tells one kind of story. As a behavioral system, "wallness" symbolizes the gradual distinction of Chinese versus "barbarian" cultures (Lattimore, 1940). What, for instance, would be the "territory" of the United States of America? Do its internal physical borders mark only one kind of border among one kind of territory making up the U.S.A. that Americans carry with them wherever they travel? Taking another illustration, what are the territories of Nestle, S.A., or Exxon, Inc., or Barclay's Bank, Ltd.? How often have we considered Western tradition as a territory?

A territory is not its boundary, just as a cell is not its membrane. But boundaries catch our attention and this is what they are designed for. As a baboon troop crosses open grasslands, a regular set of patterned behaviors mark the form of movement: infants and females cluster at the center, while adult males patrol the moving periphery. All other animals are very cognizant of that moving border. People also move in regular patterns. Visitors are constantly amazed at the smooth flow of pedestrians on the crowded streets of New York at rush hours. There is relatively little bumping or bustling. Those who are being pushed about are likely to be non-New Yorkers or noncity dwellers. Movement, then, claims a space and receives recognition. That space is also a territory.

In many species of animals the boundaries of a fixed or stationary territory will be marked in some discernible way.

Deer bite the bark from trees around the perimeter. Man constructs visible lines such as fences or walls. In more open or public places, however, territorial boundaries may appear to be less obvious. The members of a beach party hop into the surf, leaving their belongings both as objects and as arrangements that distinguish a unit of bounded space reserved for their return.

People who do not consciously see a territorial boundary nevertheless recognize it in terms of their behavior. They acknowledge a claimed space in their actions. This may be little more than a lowering or dipping of the head, the lowering of the eyes, the stroke of the hand across the forehead and hair. If they do not respect the claim for space, those who occupy the place may threaten or even attack them. Animals may display their fierce-looking canines, as in the characteristic baboon "yawn," or they may bite in the air, growl, beat their breasts, or even make mock rushes at the outsiders who approach them. Humans often glare at or speak to offenders. Ethologists have called these actions "territorial defense behaviors."

Some members of some species on some occasions hotly contest an invasion of the space they occupy. Members of other species will fall back from an invader in a characteristic behavior we often picture as meekish. Instead of threats and assaults, they use withdrawal. In so doing, they have from one vantage point yielded a hunk of turf, but from another it can be observed that they take up a position exactly similar to the one they held before the intrusion. Thus they do not hold on to a place, but they do in strategic withdrawal maintain an interpersonal distance. The space they defend is not a physical place, but instead a relative distance.

Territories may also be formed even though the parcels of space claimed are not physically occupied by people or possessions. For example, people orient their bodies in a particular direction and that orientation can lay claim to some increment of space for a period of time. The normal conventions of polite behavior dictate that a passerby should not cross directly in front of the area of a person's orientation if it can be avoided. If a group of people have formed the rough outlines of a circle and their body fronts are oriented toward one another, the unoccupied space in the center of the group nevertheless becomes a claimed territory. Others outside the circle customarily recognize the territory and avoid, if possible, crossing through the group. If it cannot be avoided, some deference will be made to the space claimed. It can be a slight lowering of the head or eyes, a curling in of the arms and shoulders, or even a voiced remark.

Ordinarily, the spaces covered by voice or gaze projection have not been considered as territories because they are temporary, even fleeting, and they do not appear to be bounded in any tangible way. Yet, if a space is claimed and that claim respected, no matter how transient the act, a territory has been formed. It may be simply the eye-holding space of a man and woman sitting across from each other; it may include all that is within the schoolteacher's view. It may also include the range of the voice. A whisper defines one space; a loud booming voice projects another. Concreteness and durability do not form essential criteria defining territory.

Obviously what is critical is that it takes a relationship of behaviors to form a territory. Unfortunately this point is frequently overlooked by those who think that each person carries around with him some personal increment of space, popularly called a "space bubble" (cf. Sommer, 1969). The "buffer zone" between two Cubans casually conversing at low density may be as small as eighteen inches. The same space under the same conditions between two Englishmen will exceed a yard. Space is defined by the joint behaviors of those present. A person may move away from another person and thus increase the interpersonal distance between them. But the distance remains a function of *both* their locations. *They* form the territory.

Distance is also a function of relationship and time. In the early stages of courtship, distance may be an issue of negotiation. But as courtship escalates, whatever the earlier distancing arrangements, the space between partners is reduced drastically. It disappears altogether in the physical union of copulation. "Personal" space becomes a dyadic space, or, if one wishes, an interpersonal space. The two lovers may later stroll in public locked arm in arm. They will move as a unit and under most conditions will be treated as a unit by passersby or those who address them. Should they part, another set of conditions may apply. One partner who recently had shared a dyadic space of zero interpersonal distance may hotly contest the approach of a stranger or other would-be suitor. And those who will resist encroachment in one situation will stand calmly next to one another jammed in a subway or as spectators at a basketball game. In short, distance is relative to affiliation and occasion, and not to the person.

Distance is relative to species and culture. Members of a troop of hippos recognize the boundaries of the range of another troop of that species when they can smell the markers of urination and defecation. But the birds and cats of that habitat show no signs of recognition, for they will cross the perimeter without hesitation. Similarly, a predator demonstrates no respect for the territorial borders of his prey. A dominant cock of one species will attack any less dominant fowl of that species who approaches him, but apparently ignores cocks of other species who walk through his region at will. In short, boundaries and the recognition of territorial borders are coded species by species. Many animals share the same habitat and their territorial borders cross and interlace one another.

Territorial behavior among humans also depends on the awareness of territorial codes. When a Cuban stands at his usual close conversational distance from an Englishman, he is unaware of the other person's sense of territory and may not even realize the Englishman is probably suffering from "territorial invasion." When members of a highly tactile cultural tradition touch those people from a nontactile tradition, discomfort or estrangement may result. What is amicable behavior to one is a violation of privacy to the other.

WAYS OF SEEING

In the *Teachings of Don Juan* (1968), Carlos Castaneda describes his mentor's teachings in terms of two realities, "ordinary" and "nonordinary." Each reality is defined by what the observer "sees." Don Juan asserted one was a continuum of the other, but "nonordinary reality" included a set of separate characteristics which enabled the observer to see more. It is as Pablo Picasso once noted: we cannot assume that to look is to see.

So it is in science. Western science evolved predominantly along a path that favored chopping things up and naming the parts. Every time a particular phenomenon was studied, the prevalent method dictated a reduction of ambiguity by isolating a few events from the total process and examining each piece separately. This method seemed to work well in physics, biology, and psychology, since there was little pressure on our learned men and women to put their Humpty Dumpties together again.

This has all changed now. Since the intellectual revolution sparked by Einstein, scientific pioneers have tried to confront complexity on its own terms, to observe and describe behavior in its natural setting and not isolated in some laboratory. Still, there remain those who wish to view nature as though it were composed solely of systems of things. Their focus is the study of cells, organs, bodies, people, buildings, stars.[2] Some biologists, for instance, persist in looking at a cell as if it were a physical object defined by its outer membrane. There are also those who would ask us to consider territory as a physical object with a boundary that defines its essential character.

Within this "thing" oriented view, our attention is directed solely at the individual and what he does. This person does this and that to another person, etc. We see action and reactions. There would be a search for cause and effect, immediate cause, sufficient cause, necessary cause, ultimate cause. We can run ourselves ragged. Harried, some people have postulated the existence of a little homunculus (an id, an instinct, a need) that is inside the individual exerting a force to keep his motor running.

But like Don Juan's nonordinary reality, there is another way of seeing, another approach, which suggests that there is a world of behaviors that cannot be explained by an object-oriented intellectual focus. If we are looking for our friend

Bill in a crowd, we search until we find him, ignoring for the most part all that is outside our immediate focus. But if there is no Bill and we wish to notice goings and comings, patterns of activities, we can simply observe clustering, dispersion, and movement independent of the physical bodies involved in the motion.[3] In the process, we do not dehumanize mankind. Quite the contrary, in discovering what he is doing, we touch on the essence of humanity. A man is not human just because he is a physical object. He is what he is by what he does. By his deeds ye shall know him.

We can observe these deeds and describe them. How we do this and how we put our observations together become our methods and theories. Our point of view, our methods are directly linked to our observations. A behavior such as eating can at one and the same time be territorial, communicational, biological, social, psychological, even, for some of us, metaphysical. It all depends on how we look at the event. It is territorial if we "see" it as territorial. It will be psychological if our perspective is psychological.

One of our goals in this book is to introduce the reader to another way of seeing. During a conversational setting, for instance, the conventions of Western tradition prescribe that we focus our attention on the speaker. Yet there is a pattern, an immediate context of such speaking that includes both the behaviors of the speaker *and* listeners—that is, the system of relations among members of the group. The next level of pattern might be the setting in which the conversation is taking place: is it among family members sitting at the dining table and conversing over a meal, or is it a group of friends who have met for a cocktail party in a living room, or is it the President's cabinet meeting in the Oval Office? As this context shifts, so does the meaning of the behavior correspondingly shift. It was Einstein who encouraged us to look at pattern in this way and not at the objects themselves.[4]

Chapter 2
PRIVACY

To some people civilization appears to be evolving in a way that systematically reduces any chance for privacy. With the rapid increase in human population and with the automobile being so much a part of our lives, one is hard put to find a secluded and private spot. We would like to believe that we can retreat into the sanctity of our own homes. But new and improved technologies bring the outside world into the privacy of our domain. We install a telephone, which, as Edmund Carpenter notes, can interrupt even the most intimate of moments. We bring television sets into our living rooms and bedrooms. We don't just passively watch TV either, for we engage in and interact with programs. We yell at the quarterback to pass. We chat with the talk shows. We go to bed and often to sleep with the television running into our lives. Jack Paar once wondered out loud to his audience how he looked between two feet.

The sense of seclusion is the feeling of privacy and we find our privacy by withdrawing, screening out, by attempting to exclude others. As the population has expanded and modern living thrown us more and more together, we have also evolved behaviors that yield some modicum of privacy, even in the most public of places. Customarily, when another couple embrace and kiss, we momentarily look away. (How many of us do exactly that when two lovers kiss on the screen?)

Behaviors become an act of privacy only when they are recognized by others. Three people talking will lower their voices so as not to intrude when one of them must answer the telephone. We don't as a matter of habit go about opening people's doors or peering in their windows, since doors, walls, and other physical devices mark a private space and define certain rights to privacy. Clothing gives one privacy in public, as do turning the body away or using arms, legs, or objects to cover parts of the body. We do not normally look into the faces of strangers, as we consider it impolite to do so. Respecting one's right to privacy means not to intrude under certain conditions, in certain ways, at certain times.

Looking is a behavior we all do thousands of times daily. Because it is such a minuscule activity in our total repertoire of activities, we pay little notice to its many fleeting uses. Yet this little behavior itself contributes to orderly relations by defining boundaries of interaction.

When strangers pass each other on an uncrowded street, they recognize each other's presence in a civil manner by momentarily glancing into each other's eyes; they will then avoid further encounter by immediately looking away. Goffman (1963) calls this pattern the ritual of civil inattention. It permits each person to acknowledge another's presence, but at the same time respects the individual's privacy. In Western culture, holding eye contact invites engagement. Looking away discourages it.

Panhandlers and prostitutes do not obey the rules of civil inattention. Instead they make an approach and attempt to hold the interaction, seeking a longer involvement. Strangers who wish to ask for the time, for a match, or for directions may also violate the rule, but they will do it with some explanation, "Excuse me, do you have the time?"

When people cross from one territory to another, they will act out a series of behaviors that customarily include the dropping of the head and eyes, as guests do when entering a home or when visitors enter an office. The lowering of the head and eyes acknowledges that they are entering someone else's territory. But the person on his own territory who perceives an intruder is unlikely to drop his eyes; instead he will stare straight ahead and demand an explanation.

People who are engaged in face-to-face conversation define a space that others outside the group are expected to respect. This respect is shown by not hearing or pretending not to hear, by not looking into the inner space, and by not barging into the middle of the group. If a person approaches a group of people talking in a relatively uncrowded place, the members of the group will usually draw closer together, splay their feet to form a circle (Goffman, 1963), and place their arms in the akimbo posture as if to bar passage into the central area. If the person approaching wishes to join the assembled group, he will pause a few feet from the group and await recognition before entering into the nucleus of the conversational arrangement.

Those people who pass by the group avoid this outer boundary. Under uncrowded conditions it is unlikely that anyone would walk through the center of the group. (Small children are often awarded rights to enter the space without being invited.) As the passerby approaches, he will look down and sometimes away, keep his hands and arms close to his body, and pass by with a quickened step. On clearing the outer boundary on the opposite side, he will resume his normal gait and posture. If the passerby has to walk through the group, he will say, "Excuse me," and look straight ahead. We call these behaviors the rite of passage (Goffman, 1963; Kendon, 1970; Scheflen, 1972).

There are spots or areas on and around the human body which may be looked at and others which are taboo. Some spots may be looked at in one instance and not in another. A woman sitting on a couch during a conversation may display her knee and calf. Within certain limits of etiquette, the other participants may be permitted to glance at, but probably not stare at, the display. She makes this specific portion of her body public. In so doing, she does not suspend the rules of privacy to include other parts of her body, nor does she invite others to touch this body spot or make comments about it. Should she notice a male staring at her breasts, she may recognize this violation by glancing at him and glancing away. She may even turn her torso in a direction away from the intruder. These acts define her claim of privacy for this area. The violator would probably be respecting her claim should he rub his eyes and turn them away from the spot, as males are accustomed to do when caught looking where they shouldn't be looking. Territorial behaviors, then, call for customary acts that define a claim for privacy as well as respect for that claim. The claim, however, is specific to the location and instance.

The rules about reaching for, looking at, and even talking at parts of the body vary. A couple in high involvement who are part of a larger conversational group may in one instance gaze into each other's eyes, lower their voices in intimacy and engage in a private conversation, and reach out and touch each other. At that moment other members of the group do not have such rights to touch them. However, these rights shift in another instance, such as the greetings that occur when another couple joins the group.

When two couples greet and exchange amenities, the rights of privacy will vary as the ceremony unfolds. All participants do not greet at the same instance. One individual may step forward and shake hands, embrace, or kiss one person from the other couple. Their partners will hold back or even look away at the moment the others touch. They themselves will not touch their partners or reach into the space occupied by the greeting pair. A temporary right of privacy is respected by the others present, including spouses and dates. As this greeting ends, the pair will step away from each other, and the process or a variation of it will be repeated until all have greeted. At the end of the salutations, the couples will then readjust their distancing to that of a conversational setting.

When Western Europeans and Americans from this background converse, they look at one another's faces. They do not look into the eyes for long. They may look out and then back into the eyes again, but this will be fleeting, for their focus is on the area around the nose and cheekbone just below the eyes. Looking longer into the eyes leads to courtship or confrontation. Lyndon Johnson's phrase, "eyeball-to-eyeball conversation," really meant face-to-face encounters in which the participants could hash out the "truth." "Look me in the eye, young man!" is an expression used by a parent in a temporary confrontation to achieve dominance and subordination. During courtship couples commonly gaze into each other's eyes. Young couples out for a stroll will repeatedly and frequently look into each other's eyes, hold the gaze, and then look away. They do so in a regular and rhythmical pattern. If they do not look away, they either kiss or break into a smile and then kiss or look away.

Those of equal status may look at spots on the face during a conversation. Not so when they are of different status. A boss stares into the face of his employee, while the employee avoids his employer's face, except to demonstrate he is listening, understanding, or agreeing. Obviously disputes can occur when the status of the participants is in doubt. The frequency of such instances is on the rise in America as more and more people of different class and ethnic backgrounds come into contact in public places and on public conveyances. The status of the people present in an elevator, on board an airplane, at a large impersonal gathering may be nebulous and individuals will employ various tactics to define themselves. But no longer is it all that easy to establish status dominance in an impersonal setting.

Friends or relatives may gaze into each other's faces. Strangers may not. Just as the panhandler intrudes by approaching and looking into the face, so does a young man who stares into the face of a young woman he does not know. A newly arrived guest at a cocktail party may quickly scan the faces of the other guests before introductions begin. He should not directly look into the faces of strangers, however, until the host introduces them.

People of high face-to-face cultures such as those of British-American or Eastern European Jewish descent may seek face-to-face looking with the notion that they are encouraging affiliation, friendship, or rapport. But if they are forcing this face-to-face behavior with Puerto Ricans, West Indians, or peoples of traditional black American experience, they risk opposite results. These cultures have quite different rules about use of the eyes and looking into faces. In black American rural and working-class traditions and in West Indian society, conversationalists do not look into one another's faces. Instead they look at imaginary spots above, below, or to the sides of the body. Looking into the eyes in black American cultures invites the escalation of a hostile encounter. Members of the culture are quite conscious of the rules about looking into the face and children are taught these rules at an early age. A mother will often chastise her son, "Get your eyes out of my face, boy!" The face in black American culture is a private spot.

In Puerto Rican culture, younger people do not look into the faces of older people, but instead keep the eyes and head cast down during the course of a conversation. Adults avoid looking into the face during conversations and may well feel dominated, embarrassed, or take evasive action if someone persists in looking into their faces. Hispanic women, however, do habitually hold eye contact, even with strange men, slightly longer than women in most other cultures. This behavior is frequently misinterpreted by non-Puerto Ricans as seductive.

During a performance actors and athletes abrogate the conventional rules about looking into and speaking into a private space and have no rights to restrict the audience's gaze. An audience may look, stare, even holler into zones normally privately reserved for the immediate participants. In the boxing or wrestling arena spectators look at all body parts and shout anything into the ring. Hissing or laughing is sometimes common during a theatrical performance. The strip-teaser exposes all regions of her body, accepting the gazes and calls as part of the act.

A performer may attempt to guide the audience's attention. The strip-tease artist momentarily freezes the focus on one part of the body only to shift that attention to another part a second later. The dancer may hold the audience for a prolonged period on his legs. But with carefully performed actions he may shift that attention to his hands and to his face. The halfback who dances and twists away from would-be tacklers will make an audience as well as team players very conscious of his legs.

While the performance is in progress, the player or performer may not call on the conventional rules against looking, but he does maintain another location for privacy. The audience may not barge into the stage or playing field. At intermission or after the performance, the actor seeks a space backstage or in the locker room private finally from public scrutiny. Guards, taboos, and other restrictions will be placed to enforce this privacy. The star performer, however, may lose this respite as he leaves the privacy of the theater.

Within the arena of the performance, certain rules of privacy do pertain. In contact sports, for instance, certain parts of the body may not be hit or grabbed. The basketball player may not be touched in the act of shooting. This rule extends as well to the uniform. In football it is not permitted to grab the opposing player by the face mask. Certain territories cannot be invaded. In between bells, a boxer may not charge into his opponent's corner. During the line-up in football, the opposing teams may not cross the line of scrimmage.

The following narration pictures the interplay of acts of privacy not as isolated examples but rather in terms of a scenario that describes people entering a scene, engaging in typical encounters, and adjusting to the arrival of newcomers.

It was an early summer's day and the beach at Marblehead, Massachusetts, was almost deserted. Soon a man we'll call Tom crossed the parking area and strolled onto the sand.

Tom walked about thirty feet and stopped. He took off his beach robe, folded it, and placed it on the sand. He sat down, removed his sunglasses and shoes, and placed these objects and a pack of cigarettes next to the robe. Tom held the territory occupied by his body and his possessions. Even under crowded conditions, spots such as these are respected as private. At the bar, for instance, we have our own location for our drink, cigarettes, and change. At home while sitting around the coffee table we and our guests have exclusive spaces for cups, dishes, and napkins.

There was a good hundred feet or so of beach between Tom and other gatherings of people. Had Tom been Hispanic or Central European he might have taken a location closer to the other clusters. They often sit or stand closer to strangers than do Americans. But Tom was clearly Irish-American: he had that characteristic ruddy hair color of the so-called "red" Irish and he carried his head and neck in the stiff position so typical of Irish-Americans.

A few moments later Tom was joined by a couple. At a distance of about ten feet or more, the new arrivals called out to Tom, who stood up and turned toward them. At that moment they dropped their eyes and heads, and walked closer. At the point at which the two men touched in handshake, they all once again dipped their heads only to immediately raise their eyes into one another's faces. Tom turned and embraced the woman. As they hugged, they kept their pelvic areas about six inches apart, as is customary in the greeting behavior of peoples from a British-American heritage. Then each party stepped back and began to talk.

Tom and the couple now formed a threesome, with Tom standing about a yard away from the man and woman and including them both in his range of focus. They, however, stood only a few inches from each other and during the conversation occasionally touched. As the three of them talked, they looked into one another's faces, but did not stare into one another's eyes. Nor, for that matter, did they look at one another's lower bodies.

As one point the woman glanced down the beach at a man sitting alone. As his eyes raised to meet hers, they both looked away. Some moments later they both repeated this act. This pattern continued for a few seconds when her two companions must have sensed something for they turned and looked at the man, who rather ostentatiously turned away to watch the ocean. The little territory between the two strangers crumbled with the preemptory rights of another territorial claim.

Tom remained standing near his possessions. He thus held two kinds of physical space; for he stood in one area while reserving an adjacent area for his possessions. But he also

used a third kind of space, the space that was occupied by
the orientation of his body and the projection of his voice.
While Tom could lay a claim to space immediately around
him for his body and gestures, his space of orientation could
include the immediate conversational setting, or it could include also a huge vista as when Tom would scan the beach.

At any one moment Tom stood in an area of about eighteen inches, but as he talked he would shift his position within
the larger space of about a yard. At times he would step toward the couple as if to emphasize a point. At times he would
step back to increase the space of the conversational group.
From time to time he shifted to the right and then to the
left, utilizing a space wider than his physical size required.
This behavior helped confirm that Tom was Irish-American,
for people with an ancestry from the British Isles or Northern
Europe use about a square yard of space when in normal
conversation in uncrowded conditions. But this three-foot distancing was not Tom's "personal space." It was a conversational area used jointly by the couple *and* Tom. Even this
conventional spacing is relative to the situation and character
of the affiliation. The man and woman, for instance, stood
closer together, sharing a location roughly equal to the one
held by Tom alone.[1]

At no time during the course of the conversation did Tom
reach into or step into the space occupied by the couple. Nor
did they into his. The two equal-sized locations for standing
functioned as temporary private territories. The projection of
voices, gestures, and gaze operated according to other rules of
privacy. They avoided looking at certain spots on the body,
especially the lower regions of the torso. They projected their
voices specifically into the space between them, and their
voice levels obviously did not include other people on the
beach.

A young teen-age boy approached the threesome. They
were engrossed in conversation and the boy paused at a customary threshold some three feet away from them. He did
not speak out with a greeting. However, his hesitation was
momentary, for almost at the instant of hesitation Tom
caught his eye, turned, and reached out to include him. Tom

put his arm around the young man's shoulder and drew him into the group. They did not shake hands, but exchanged a few words of greeting. As Tom dropped his arm from the boy's shoulder, each member of the group stepped back a few inches, forming a foursome, and resumed the conversation.[2]

After the circle was enlarged, the couple stepped away from each other and no longer stood at such a close distance. While they still stood closer to each other than to the other members of the group, each now clearly held separate locations. The foursome formed a circle with about a square yard of open space in the center.[3] This center acted as an area into which the members projected their voices, gestures, and frequently gazes. An imaginary peripheral boundary at their backs defined the group's immediate private territory. But within the total space claimed by the foursome, smaller private territories were claimed by the individual members.

As the morning passed on the beach at Marblehead, more and more family members arrived. The greeting ritual with several variations for affinity, sex, and age was repeated with each new arrival. By the late morning some twenty people occupied the family's territory on the beach. Within this larger space, however, various members gathered into several smaller clusters. To a certain degree the activities of any one cluster were private from the others. Tom and another man sat face to face and talked. The couple by now stood a few yards away and conversed with another couple. Closer to the water lay two young lovers facing and touching each other. An older man sat alone watching the waves, but obviously listening to the chatter of the children near by. The younger children played in the sand a little distance from these four clusters. Still farther from the water, three women engaged in preparing food for the assembly.

Each cluster was engaged in some activity, either eating, daydreaming, conversing, playing, or courting. While the younger children at times walked through any area, adults did not. Each cluster apparently was defined by the activity.

There were spaces for eating, playing, conversing. Like the family home, the area on the beach collectively claimed by

Tom's family constituted a total base of operations, but individual operations went on within the whole. Each had specific rules of privacy and ways of dealing with intrusions. In the home the spaces are marked by physical barriers such as walls and furniture. Here on the beach they were bounded temporarily only by the conventional behaviors of Tom and his family.

The behaviors Tom's family used to achieve some privacy on an open beach are replicated in more concrete and visible means by hedges, fences, walls, and doors of permanently constructed territories. Tom's family would employ the backs of their bodies, elbows, arms, and eye avoidance to protect the privacy of the inner circle of conversational activity. Other physical barriers do the same in defining the private territory of a household and private territories within the household.

The Smiths, for example, own a comfortable house on two acres of land in a well-to-do suburban community. Not counting a double garage, a finished basement, and three and a half baths, their home has twelve rooms. In form it is similar to the public gathering of Tom's family on the beach. Around the space occupied by Tom's family were imaginary boundaries that outsiders were expected to respect. They were not to peer into, project their voices into, or walk into the space claimed by Tom's family. But such rules will be conditioned by crowding and other factors of public interaction. The boundaries of the Smith property in contrast are much more visible, fixed, and inviolable. And the physical barriers of the house itself define the Smiths' territory as being distinctly more private than that of the family on the beach.

Each room in the house is laid out as a separate cluster of space that is used according to the traditions of modern middle-class living. The laundry room, dining room, adult bedroom, study, and part of the kitchen are areas typically limited to a single purpose: washing, eating, sleeping, writing, cooking. But the living room, den, rumpus room, and adolescent bedrooms usually are set aside for several kinds of activities. In the living room the Smiths have arranged the furniture for conversation and for watching TV, while the rumpus room is arranged for play, TV watching, reading, sewing. The children's bedrooms serve as play areas, study areas, sleeping areas, conversational areas, etc. The large family kitchen is really two rooms, an unpartitioned area that has one zone for cooking and cleaning and one zone for eating.

The setup in each room is fixed according to the activities of that room. In the living room two sofas face each other across a coffee table. At one end there is a large stuffed chair. This U-shaped arrangement forms a nucleus for conversation. Back against the wall at the other end of the seats is a TV. The chair and sofas then can also become a place for watching television. The two sofas provide two separate side-by-side seating arrangements so that three people seated on one sofa can face a similar element across a central space taken up by the coffee table. Just as rules marked the behaviors of side-by-side versus face-to-face formations in the standing clusters at Tom's family gathering, so does the furniture layout arrange participants, defining in part the character of many of their behaviors.

In the dining area six chairs are gathered around a rectangular shaped table. The two end seats are equipped with armrests and are reserved for Mr. and Mrs. Smith. The other four chairs are armless. The dining room in the Smith household is used almost exclusively for the evening meal and on formal dining occasions. In other households, especially in the less affluent examples, the dining table may be used for additional activities such as card playing or writing. The total setup forms a nucleus for face-to-face and side by side dinner conversation. It defines the single private spaces for Mr. and Mrs. Smith and the smaller shared locations on the sides for guests and the children. This setup arranges people in a setting similar in form to the conversational rings that occurred on the beach.

In the kitchen two areas are defined, one for eating which duplicates the dining area and one for food preparation and cleanup. In the latter area we find a variation of the typical American kitchen work space. On one side of the room are a row of cabinets, a counter top, and an oven. Across a relatively wide space, a similar module of more cabinets, another counter top, a refrigerator, and dishwasher line the opposite wall. In one sense these two modules face each other. But the open center space is not the focus as it is in the dining and living rooms. In contrast, there is a centripetal direction in which the individual faces not the center but instead the counters or cabinets along the wall.

The master bedroom has a full bath, a vanity alcove, two large walk-in closets, two dressers, and a double bed. Each of the three children has a separate bedroom with a bed, closet space, chest of drawers, small study desk, and shelves for hi-fi sets or odds and ends. There is also a guest room with a bed, night stand, and chest of drawers.

Within each room there are areas that are considered more private than others. Closets and drawers are more private than open spaces in the bedrooms. A guest sitting at the kitchen table talking to Mrs. Smith can look at the cabinets and counter tops along the walls. But cabinet and refrigerator doors prevent that guest from peering into the more private areas of Mrs. Smith's kitchen. Similarly, some rooms will be considered more private than others. As drawers and closet doors mark private zones within a room, so do walls, doors, and stairways define different degrees of privacy. In the Smith home the dining room is separated from the living room by an open doorway, while a swinging door closes the kitchen off from the dining room. Within limits guests can freely occupy these rooms, thereby making the first floor of the Smith house relatively public. But the stairs, hallway, and closed doors of the second floor mark this as a more private region. The outer walls of the house and property boundaries define yet another type of privacy which includes the conventional rules respecting property rights.

Private dwellings, then, are arranged so that one moves through public communal locations to increasingly private zones. Any household member or invited guest, for instance, can move freely from the entrance area of the front door and center hall into the main zones of the living room. By asking, guests may also use the toilet in the downstairs powder room. The Smiths may also invite guests into their eat-in kitchen, dining room, den, or sometimes even the rumpus room. Mr. Smith's study, the basement, and the upstairs area remain zones normally reserved for the exclusive use of the Smith family. Guests will not wander into these rooms and the Smiths will probably invite them into one room only for a specific reason.

Some rooms within the Smith house have been set aside as areas private from some or all other family members. On the upstairs floor Mrs. Smith has a small room commonly referred to as a sewing room, which she uses to store odds and ends and to retreat to from time to time. The family respects this area as her room. Similarly Mr. Smith has a study on the main floor, which, while other family members use it sometimes, is recognized as his private work area. The master bathroom is off limits to the children. The adults do not use or at least do not bathe in the other two bathrooms. If any bedroom is occupied and the door closed, all other family members, including adults, hesitate to enter.

All private locations are subject to violation, of course, in accordance with time schedules and special circumstances. During a house party a guest may use an upstairs bathroom if the powder room is occupied. The teen-age daughter may use the stove either when Mother isn't home or when she isn't cooking for the family. The dining table usually has fixed and assigned locations for each member of the family, but should the family not be eating, one may sit where he pleases. Generally, although the closets and drawers in the children's bedroom are private, Mom may open them to put freshly laundered clothes inside. Siblings are unlikely to have rights even to enter the room of another sibling. One frequent object in the American middle-class home is the poster or sign on the door of a teen-ager's room announcing in bold letters, "KEEP OUT!"

The Robinson family lives in a five-room ghetto apartment in the inner city. They have six children. The four boys occupy one bedroom, which is outfitted with two bureaus, one closet, and two double beds. Two boys sleep in each bed. The parents have one bedroom to themselves and the two girls occupy a third. The ghetto apartment has no dining room. The family must eat in the kitchen, but it by no means approaches the size of the Smith family's eat-in kitchen.

In the Robinson kitchen there is one module of counter, cabinets, and stove along one wall, a module of refrigerator and cabinets on the other. At one end is a doorway. At the other is a small space holding a table; the table is about the size of the middle-class card table. There are three chairs arranged about the table. A fourth chair is pressed against the wall behind the table, as there is no room available to use it. The Robinsons must eat in shifts.

In the Robinson living room there is a sofa along one wall, a TV across the room on the second, an overstuffed chair on the third. The entrance area and a small table with a vase for flowers take up the space along the fourth wall. When the family watches television, four members sit on the three cushioned couch, one in the stuffed chair, and the others on the floor. The boys do their homework in the adjoining hallway or occasionally at the kitchen table. The crowded small bedrooms are used almost exclusively for sleeping. When there is company, then homework, TV watching, and conversation occur in the same area. Put in other terms, the small living room is the only space where for all practical purposes the family functions together, and the degree of privacy that the household members have from each other is thus extremely limited.[4]

As people go about their daily activities they observe rules of etiquette that separate events and define different degrees of privacy. Just as Tom and his family obeyed the rules of privacy during their gathering on an open and public beach, so do family members observe these rules in the privacy of their homes. The structure of the house, however, defines a different degree of privacy than could occur on the beach. Within the home, separate activities gain privacy from other activities by virtue of the behaviors of the household members and also from the structures of walls, doors, and rooms. In most American homes, for example, it is improper for teenage children to pass between parents or guests when they are talking. If they are not participants in the adult conversation, they do not project their voices into the conversational space. But separation and privacy become more absolute when adults enter a different room and close the door or when children are sent outside to play. But whether it is a wall or a rule of behavior, the goal of defining privacy, of gaining recognition of a territory, is the same. In fact, walls and other built structures are extensions of the much older rules of human interaction.

Chapter 3
INTRUSIONS

Modern life is crowded: we are ever more frequently and regularly passing by, standing and sitting with, and talking to strangers. Jamming in like sardines on the subway, sitting three abreast for six hours on an airplane, lining up ten deep to watch the Parade of Roses, dodging pushcarts in a supermarket, walking three blocks on any busy urban sidewalk are all daily occurrences. And each of these events requires some momentary interaction, even if this is just a recognition of the presence of others.

People are not usually conscious of these acts. Brushing the hand across the forehead, pulling the arms in against the body, or lowering the head seem insignificant because they are habitual. Yet body movements are as important as words. They help maintain privacy, reduce or increase the chances of engagement, and prevent intrusions.

Conventions of pedestrian etiquette, for example, prescribe that strangers do not touch one another on the street. In New York, one of the more "impersonal" cities of America, people who bump into each other on the crowded sidewalks rarely fail to apologize. Yet a person from a sparsely populated region of southern Illinois might be startled at being bumped on a Manhattan street corner and complain about the very abrupt apology. What seems abrupt to the urban neophyte is, in the context of living in a densely populated environment, sufficient for the occasion. It also avoids a prolonged encounter, something more familiar to the small-town inhabitant where sidewalks are less crowded and collisions much less frequent. Just as the person from southern Illinois walks according to a shared pattern of pedestrian movement in his region, so do pedestrians living in Chicago, New York, London, Munich, and Moscow customarily walk in such a way that their movements are predictable and intrusions infrequent.[1]

Collisions do occur, however, and the reaction to the intrusions varies quite markedly from city to city. Londonites, for instance, go to considerable effort to avoid touching or bumping into each other, and if a collision does occur, they apologize. The pattern is similar in New York, but less striking. In Paris, however, people bump into each other rather frequently, as if they made no effort to avoid the contact, and do not usually apologize. During the winter when the streets are slippery, Muscovites often fall, crash into each other, and sometimes bring down a whole group of people like a stack of dominoes. They rarely apologize and pay little attention to those who fall. In New York and Munich, in contrast, slipping is a much rarer event as de-icing salt is regularly strewn about. When it does occur, it is the cause of much concern.

Speaking in a soft or loud voice can also prevent or provoke intrusion. In America, people in a public restaurant usually confine their voices to the table at which they are sitting, so that their conversation does not carry to adjoining tables. Those people who do speak loudly seem exhibitionistic, since they apparently wish to call attention to themselves. There are, of course, those other instances where people deliberately offend and disturb those around them. Groups of teen-agers frequently seek to shock their elders or gain some reaction from them. Workmen at a construction site may indulge in overt exhibitionistic behavior apparently as a form of crude entertainment for onlookers, especially if those spectators are female.

Everyday behavior protects us from the penetration of touch, gaze, gesticulation, and voice. If a group of people are assembled on a street corner to greet one another or hold a brief conversation, those who pass by respect the space claimed by the assembly. Passersby look down and away and give as wide a berth to the group as density and location allow. Yet in certain places some people peer directly into the group as if to determine what they are doing.

Such behavior occurs on the streets of Munich where older residents, especially older women, noticeably stare into the space of a conversing group. The same behavior occurs in some of the traditional Italian-American neighborhoods of New York, in Rome, Boston, San Juan, and probably most other traditional residential urban neighborhoods in the Western world. Older residents make it their business to peer into any sidewalk assemblies as if to monitor what is going on in their territory. From one perspective this rather aggressive behavior intrudes on the rights of privacy during a public assembly. From another it can be seen as part of a larger pattern controlling the goings and comings in a neighborhood. When the streets are watched, the streets are protected (Jacobs, 1961 and Newman, 1972). And it is a traditional role of older people to monitor what is going on in their neighborhood.

Nevertheless, the intrusion of staring can make us feel uncomfortable, and should it continue we probably will begin to take some sort of counteraction. Unfortunately, sometimes staring may be an unwitting violation committed by someone from a different cultural or ethnic background who either is not familiar with customary gazing behavior or is intrigued by the novelty of what he sees. European tourists visiting America often stare at the unfamiliar sight of Orientals or couples of mixed racial backgrounds. In turn, American tourists in Mexico are notorious offenders who stare at peasant Indians from the countryside. The person whose space is being violated may not take such a gratuitous attitude about the offense. He might conclude that people who do not obey the rules of eye space may not observe other rules as well. There is yet no justification for this position. With very few exceptions, most of the many thousands of minor little intrusions of eye space that occur daily in any large city end right there.

Let us return to Marblehead Beach. When the young man joined Tom and the couple, he did not take a position in the middle of the conversational circle, but instead stood at a point between Tom and the couple. He did not step in between the man and woman, since people normally do not separate those who identify themselves as being with each other. With the exception of the man and woman who stood closer together, there was no touching or stepping into the space occupied by another. Had the participants been of French or Eastern European descent, a great deal of touching would have occurred. In contrast to the conversational group, however, a great deal of touching, stroking, and kissing took place with the young lovers near by. Their actions were not violations of privacy, for the lovers had abrogated the customary rules of spacing and physical intrusion in favor of courtship.[2]

As the morning passed, more and more of Tom's family arrived at the beach. But aside from the conventions of greeting new arrivals, Tom and the other three maintained their conversation for a while. At one point a young boy about five or six years old walked directly into the center of the circle and spoke to Tom. It was a brief exchange and, while the adults tolerated this intrusion into their conversational space, Tom reached out, placing his arm on the young boy's shoulder, and gently drew him closer to him and out of the center of the conversational area. Had the youngster been older, it would have been extremely unlikely that the group would have permitted him to interrupt as he did and to take such a central position. Children learn the rules of privacy and intrusion from infancy, but mandatory compliance is not expected until they reach five to seven years age.

In open public spaces like the beach, people must define territories with their bodies, personal belongings, and behaviors. Inside a building or public conveyance, walls, doors, and seating arrangements reinforce these behaviors. On board an airplane, for instance, all seats are arranged side by side in rows that face the front. Each row in coach provides three passengers with a small semi-private module. (In first class there are two seats in a row.) Each row is open on the aisle side, but is closed off on the other three sides by the inside wall of the machine and by the front and back of the seats. This arrangement restricts people sitting to the front and back from intruding by touch, gaze, and to a lesser extent by voice. Within each module the passengers sitting side by side have some freedom of gaze without intruding into the space of a neighbor. There are also spaces to the front and below the seat for arm and leg movement. Additional privacy is gained through behaviors similar to those employed on the beach:

Mr. Winfield boards the jet to Los Angeles, hoping for a peaceful flight and a row of seats to himself. As he locates his seat he glances across the aisle at a young couple. The woman is sitting next to the window with her head slightly lowered while she thumbs through a magazine. Her companion has turned his body partially to face her. Their postures reduce the view into their inner circle of space. Mr. Winfield settles into his window seat, places his briefcase in the center seat, and starts to read a book.

As the plane fills up, he pretends not to notice the incoming passengers. To his chagrin someone pauses and looks at him. He returns the glance and both look away. The new arrival takes the aisle seat and places his newspaper on top of Mr. Winfield's briefcase. A few moments later they both feel the presence of a third person standing at the edge of their module, but they avoid eye contact and do not raise their heads to acknowledge his presence. This act proves of no avail, however, for the man says, "Excuse me, but I believe this is my seat." The seated pair have no recourse but to remove their possessions and yield to the claim for the center location. The three strangers thus become closely arranged in a side-by-side pattern and each takes care not to reach into the space directly in front of his neighbor.

The new arrival smiles at Mr. Winfield, who in turn nods and looks away. He says something about the weather and Mr. Winfield replies politely and returns to his book. The man in the center removes a letter from his pocket and all three passengers proceed to involve themselves in their respective private activities: they lower their heads and eyes, orient their bodies toward the front, and focus on the objects in their hands. But only a short time elapses before each starts to steal glances into the other's space. Mr. Winfield glances at the letter and then quickly back to his book. His neighbor glances over at the book and then back to the letter. They avoid eye contact and take great pains not to be caught staring. In so doing they respect the relative privacy of each seating location.

During the course of the flight the other two men occasionally chat and, as they become acquainted, the rules against intrusion are relaxed to allow each to look at and talk into the space claimed by the other. Touching, however, remains constrained.

The seating arrangement and the respective behaviors of the three men give each a little privacy. The one major zone of contention is the armrest which overlaps the region of two separate seating locations. There is room really for only one elbow and Mr. Winfield and his neighbor quickly become engaged in a small unobtrusive war for sole possession of the armrest. It is never resolved. At moments one gives way to temporary possession by the other, only to make a claim again some minutes later.

In the open seating of the airplane, train, or bus, passengers must accommodate themselves to the public nature of the travel. Total privacy is impossible. Had the passengers been traveling by ship, the territorial arrangements would have differed. One can retreat into the privacy of a cabin. Other passengers would not enter except on invitation. Of course, some other adjustments would have to be reached if the cabin were shared with others: each passenger would get a private area for sleeping and the storage of personal belongings, but the shower and lavatory would have to be shared. In Western society, strangers traveling together usually arrange use of a shared location according to some mutually agreed upon schedule that prevents potential conflicts and intrusions. Just as the occupants of a cabin know the schedule of the steward's rounds in the morning, so do they work out an agreement of use among themselves about shared facilities. In fact, this element of scheduling or turn-taking is a common feature of many territorial arrangements. On board the aircraft, passengers are obliged to wait their turn by lining up for use of the lavatory. Americans habitually line up to catch a bus, to purchase tickets at the theater, to mail a package at the post office.

There are similar rules for using the streets in most cities. In some neighborhoods of the city, public pathways are used at one time of the day and week by nonresidents who must pass through on their way to and from work. At other times residents claim the sidewalks and streets for their use for shopping and playing. Affluent commuters readily drive through a slum neighborhood daily, but would hesitate to pass through on a Sunday drive. Correspondingly, the ghetto residents tolerate the commuter traffic but would probably be annoyed at the same drivers barging through their sole space for play on weekends. In the past when ethnic and class boundaries were more rigid in American cities, minority group peoples could use the public pathways of wealthier white people only at certain times of the day and under certain conditions. A black person, for instance, ran the risk of being accosted should he be passing through a white neighborhood late at night.

The traditionally rich Rittenhouse Square area of Philadelphia is a residential space about four blocks wide in a north-south direction. Immediately south of this wealthy residential neighborhood is a black ghetto section which years ago housed the servants of the rich. Just to the north of Rittenhouse Square lies a shopping district and a subway system. In the morning and evening blacks regularly moved from the ghetto through the Rittenhouse Square section on their way to the homes where they were employed or on their way to the subway. In the later morning and midafternoon these streets would be almost exclusively occupied by the white residents of the district who were strolling, visiting, or shopping.

Formerly it would have been considered an intrusion for blacks to walk, loiter, or sit in this part of Philadelphia during the midmorning or early afternoons. Up to about ten years ago such intruders were likely to be accosted by residents or by police. Almost anyone, however, could enter the Rittenhouse Square area at any time of the day were his costume or his props appropriate to a mission of service. Various and sundry delivery or pickup personnel, maintenance men, plumbers, electricians, and telephone service men were they to comport themselves correctly would be granted rights of access without challenge. Similarly, government service personnel, such as police, firemen, and sanitation men, moved freely through the neighborhood in the course of their duties.

In the evening the Rittenhouse Square neighborhood would become the almost exclusive domain of the residents. The presence of black Americans in this area in the late evening would have been the cause for surveillance and monitoring of their movements. Should they have been found loitering, they were likely to have been challenged as to their purpose for being in the neighborhood.

In the past few years, of course, these arrangements have changed. It is now commonplace for black Americans, as well as other nonresidents, to visit the restaurants of the Rittenhouse Square area, to use the sidewalks and streets as transit zones at all times of the day and night, and to stroll through the small central square. A few years ago any non-conservative-looking youth or minority-group person would have felt uncomfortable had he entered the square and taken up a location on a bench. He would definitely have felt the overt surveillance behavior of the others and had he remained there for some time probably would have been approached by a passing policeman. Today the police occasionally patrol the square and observe the activities of youths and blacks, but for the most part they leave them alone.

Intrusion, therefore, is not simply a matter of physical presence in a territory, but also a question of presence at a certain time of the day, week, or year. It also includes some public statement of purpose or mission through uniforms or other displays of behavior. As we have seen in America and elsewhere, what constitutes an intrusion at one point in history becomes a rightful and legal pattern in another. We have yet to witness, however, the time when all citizens have been granted the same rights of privacy or the same unobscured rights to access. Intrusions are related to ideology, law, and politics.

In order for us to gain an understanding of how people use space within the home, the authors asked families in the Bronx borough of New York and in the suburban section of Westchester County to the north for permission to place three television cameras in their apartments and houses. One camera was located in the kitchen, another in the living room, and the third in the hallway. The cameras remained in some households for weeks, and even months. In others the duration of study lasted for much shorter periods. We were thus able to learn how people actually used space, as opposed to their telling us how they used that space.[3]

In each household all members, including children, had spaces for the storage of personal items such as clothing, mementos, etc. In theory these spaces were invulnerable from the intrusion of other household members. In practice we witnessed more than just the incidental violation of private space. Siblings opened and looked inside drawers and removed one another's clothing and other personal belongings. This was frequently a source of bitter verbal, and sometimes violent, conflict. Teen-age girls demanded privacy from the intrusions of other siblings and especially their mother. Nevertheless, whenever they wished, mothers rarely hesitated to inspect the private spaces of their daughters. Parents took it as part of their duties and rights to maintain perfunctory control over the total lives of their children. In turn, children who invaded the private domain of adults would be scolded or reprimanded for doing so.

Obviously, to some extent each household establishes its own rules of privacy and intrusion. What may be a violation in one household may not be in another. But we should not make too much of individual differences, for, after all, each is part of larger social and cultural traditions. There are clear similarities that appear in all households within a particular class or ethnic group. There are very different circumstances for the availability of private space for children as we move up the economic ladder. In the suburban household children are more likely to have their own bedroom and as well other rather secure private locations within that bedroom or elsewhere in the house. The latter can range from a locked box in the back of a closet to rotating hiding places about the bedroom. The young teen-age girl who hides the love letters from her boyfriend in a sock in an old tennis shoe in her closet knows of the potential intrusion of her mother. But she also has the space hopefully to avert that intrusion. The young boy who experiments at masturbation behind the closed door of his own bedroom expects no immediate threat of intrusion. But in the crowded ghetto apartment in which a youngster must share a room with one, two, or three other siblings, the threat of intrusion is always imminent. Similarly the limited space about the room provides little opportunity for a secret private location. The private location awarded the child for his or her personal belongings is much more subject not only to the intrusions of the mother but other household members as well.

Definitions of privacy and problems of intrusion within the home also arise from furniture arrangements and their use. Most notable examples will be found in the dining areas and living rooms. Many families in America customarily provide each member with a particular chair in a particular location at the dining table. At meal after meal the family will regularly arrange themselves according to the pattern. Even in the absence of a member, such as a parent at lunch time, the members present will typically sit in their "own" chairs. Occasionally young children may argue to sit in Father's or Mother's chair and some negotiations will have to take place should the children quarrel to sit in the absent parent's chair. But even if the child is permitted to sit in Dad's location, everyone overtly recognizes the exception and notes it as a temporary deviation.

The tradition of having an individual chair for each parent and child is quite a bourgeois thing in America and Western Europe. In poorer households, especially in overcrowded so-called slum neighborhoods, there are often too few chairs for each family member to have the luxury of claiming one for his individual use. In some households it is physically impossible, both from lack of space and lack of chairs, for family members to eat together or sit together at a family meal. Household members may have to eat at various locations in the apartment or in shifts. Some individuals may not sit down at all, but eat while moving about the apartment, carrying food with them as they walk.

A similar problem arises in the living room. Many Americans consider living-room chairs to be private locations. Others are less direct in their claims. If Granddad lives with the family, he may well have his own chair that the family avoids in all instances. But for the other members living-room chairs frequently become personal property to be claimed at certain times of the day for certain situations. It is common in poor and middle-class households to arrange a sofa and chairs in front of the television set. During the evening one of these seats will usually be occupied by Father and another by Mother, with the other seats in the room taken up by the children. But during the day when Father is not at home a child will sit in Dad's chair.

The extent to which a living-room seat will be considered private and how a claim will be treated vary by class and culture. Puerto Rican children frequently sit in Dad's chair when he is out of the room. As they hear him approach the living room, they immediately get up and move to another location. In working-class black American families, the child does not always leave the adult chair until requested to do so. In those poorer Puerto Rican households without sufficient chairs or sofas for all family members, adults claim their sitting spaces and then children will crowd together in remaining seats or on the living-room floor. In a similar apartment occupied by a black American family, adult males often seem reluctant or unwilling to move their children out of the seat and would leave the room and sometimes the apartment instead.

Thus in situations of scarcity, such as insufficient seating, the cultural values of intrusion, and in this instance coupled with attitudes toward the position of children, become significant factors explaining human conduct. The Puerto Rican father who walks into a room to find an empty spot on the

couch, the white working-class father who gently but firmly
eases his young son out of his chair, and the black father
who in finding all seating locations occupied turns and leaves
the room operate under different codes of values, codes that
are not easily transferred across ethnic lines.

Chairs and other locations in the household do not always
belong to a particular person, but instead to a particular role.[4]
In one Puerto Rican household, for instance, the family had
placed a sectional sofa in front of the TV set. Evening after
evening father and mother sat in the center of the sofa with
their young son sitting to his father's left at one end and a
younger daughter sitting to her mother's right at the other
end. On the surface, it would appear that each person had
his or her own seating location. Thus the seat at the far right
could be referred to as little Margarita's. But an interesting
event took place that illustrates the real-life complexities as
compared with the simplicity of our generalizations about
that life.[5]

One day the young boy was running through the living
room when he sharply struck his shin on the coffee table. He
yelled out in pain and fell to the floor. Mother immediately
dashed in from the kitchen and lifted him to the sofa. She
placed the boy on the far right of the sofa, in little Margarita's "spot," even though she had to carry him the few
steps past his usual seat. Mother rubbed her son's shin and
offered her sympathy. A few moments later she reminded him
in a teasing voice that he was a big boy and should bear the
discomfort. She gently pushed him up and out of the seat. He
limped about for a moment and then sat down on the far left
of the sofa. But mother appeared to ignore him and returned
to the kitchen. Little Margarita's "seat" then was not just reserved for Margarita, but was also a location for the activity
of mothering. When that activity was completed, the boy was
an intruder who was playfully pushed out of his sister's seat.

The claim made on certain locations in the household can
also be a result of time of day. Mom may allow her son to
putter near her in the kitchen during the afternoon, but as the
time of the evening meal approaches she may consider his
presence an intrusion on the space she needs to prepare sup-

per. In one black family a ceremony was held in the kitchen just about every Saturday morning. The children of the family gathered here throughout the morning while a friend of the father cut their hair. He worked at a barber shop during the weekdays, but would come every Saturday to cut the hair of various family members, as well as other friends and relatives.

During the morning haircutting, other friends of the father (we'll call the father Jim) would also gradually appear and joke with the children. At noon, however, the children were shunted out of the room and the kitchen changed into an adult domain. The children confined themselves to other rooms or went outdoors.

A seventeen-year-old niece of Jim's named Helen lived in the household. On Saturday morning Helen would sit in the kitchen playing with the other children while flirting with her uncle's friends. At noon she regularly joined the other children's exit from the kitchen, leaving the location for the adults. One Satuday, however, at about the noon hour, all the children's hair had been cut, but Helen was still holding court, so to speak, with Jim's friends. She was sitting at the head of the kitchen table in Jim's normal location at dinnertime talking to two men. Suddenly Jim emerged from the living room and struck her, knocking her off the chair. Everyone present was stunned. Slowly Helen got up and left the room, whereupon Jim sat down in his usual location and started conversing with his friends.

All were extremely surprised at his action, including Jim. He was a very mild-mannered person and certainly not prone to violence. We never saw him punish his children by physical means. Helen was equally surprised, for she enjoyed a warm relationship with her uncle. The family was at a loss to explain his behavior. Was this, then, an idiosyncratic act on Jim's part? Jim's behavior might have been the result of his anger over Helen's flirtations and it reached a climax that particular Saturday. But like many psychological interpretations, this conclusion requires knowing what Jim himself did not know. Instead we saw the event as a simple territorial violation, unusual in the household's regular routine and therefore sparking a sharp if idiosyncratic reaction. Helen had occupied a chair into the afternoon which she could claim only in the morning. Whatever the excuse, flirting, eating, or talking, she had acted in a position beyond her time.

In poorer neighborhoods, there is the sad problem of people clinging to traditional uses of space and rules of intrusion that are mere hangovers from earlier days. Parents in many ghetto apartments try to use the living room as if it were the parlor of an older rural American house that was rarely used except when special guests entered the house. Close friends and relatives would more likely be entertained in the living room or, as was the custom in working-class homes, in the kitchen. When some families made the move from rural America to the less spacious confines of urban tenements, they attempted to maintain the parlor custom. Unfortunately, there is no other space for family use in the tenement apartment, except in some rare cases the kitchen. This cultural value is simply unmanageable in the physical confines of urban ghetto living. Nevertheless, in a couple of households children would endlessly enter the living room as the only possible space to spread out and just as endlessly be reprimanded for intruding into a forbidden territory.

In the small ghetto apartment, multiple activities often must be carried out in the small living room at the same time. Some members might be talking to visitors, others watching television, others playing, and still others doing homework. By traditional middle-class standards each of the activities would be intruding on the other. In the suburban home, a child would be expected to do his homework in his room; children at play would be sent to their room or a rumpus room; and those who wanted to watch television would retire to a family room or den. When such separate and private areas do not exist, activities must occur in one common room. The noise level is often high and most of us would find it disconcerting. In the poorer households which we studied, however, the people *did not act* as if the intrusions disturbed them.

There were times when the spatial confines of the over-crowded and small ghetto apartment resulted in overt disturbances. In one household the mother did not permit the children in the kitchen while she was cooking. When the cooking chores had been completed, she would then leave the tiny kitchen and go to her own bedroom. The children could only then enter the kitchen and go to the stove, serve themselves, and by eating in shifts could sit on the two chairs located by the small kitchen table. If a child attempted to enter the kitchen while the mother was still cooking, she would scold him and occasionally even strike him. The children often congregated at the threshold waiting for the mother to be finished and not daring to intrude on her temporary private space.

Sometimes the very size of the ghetto apartment forces improvisations that negate the usual rules of room intrusions. For example, it is not uncommon to find a child's bedroom in the kitchen. In one household, a family of seven occupied two rooms, and the living room became a dormitory for five teen-age boys. Some families evolved rules of intrusion that held for certain hours of the day. If a child's bedroom was in the living room and his bedtime was nine o'clock, then, at nine, watching television and talking ended. The room was converted into a sleeping area and the child could no longer treat the room as a play or living area. Most households found it impossible to maintain any sense of room privacy, as family members would sometimes roam about the apartment at all times of the day or night for one reason or the other.

People living in the poorer sections of the city also share the very real threat of strangers intruding on the private space of the family's living quarters. One such type of intruder is the burglar and it is a regular and frightening experience for those who live in the ghetto. Black people complain bitterly about such events in their neighborhood, mainly because crime continues at such a high level year after year. Puerto Rican families are continually preoccupied with burglary and other break-ins. Many Puerto Ricans fear not only the intrusions of outsiders but also, sometimes with justification, the intrusions of superintendents and other personnel who may work in the apartment house. Their fear focuses on robbery and especially on rape.

In most larger apartment buildings in New York there are

some staff personnel whose function is to maintain the building. One common rule of privacy is that the staff not enter residents' apartments without invitation, except possibly in the event of some emergency. Similarly residents are not to invade certain private areas set aside for the staff. There are common spaces which include the hallways, lobby, elevators, laundry areas, etc.

The problem with these communal areas is that they are sometimes invaded by persons who are neither staff nor resident. In the luxury apartments, owners combat this problem by increasing staff, television monitoring, increased lighting, and locking certain areas after dark. In the ghetto household, the corridors, roofs, basements, and fire escapes become areas marked by considerable mugging and other violence. These zones are often feared more than the streets. It is not uncommon for parents to forbid their children to enter the hallways unescorted, let alone to play on the roof or in the alleyways.

Intrusion occurs in other wider contexts as well. Traditionally in America an urban neighborhood would likely be occupied almost exclusively by the people of one ethnic background or class. Large sections of a city would be inhabited by Italian-, Jewish-, or Irish-Americans. Other sections would be held by the very rich, others by the middle class, and still others would be the old tenement districts of the city. But since about 1920, there has been an increasing migration of blacks and Puerto Ricans into blocks which were formerly the domain of European ethnic groups. Elaborate attempts over the past several decades to prevent free movement of blacks and Puerto Ricans into certain neighborhoods have resulted in a rapid rise in racism and some violence.

An intrusion most hated by all concerned was that of block busting. In the former practice, whites would pose as potential renters or buyers and, after having obtained the housing, a minority person would in fact move in.

Unscrupulous real estate speculators would then attempt to gain control of the property at ridiculously low prices and then in turn pass on the property to a minority group member at a much higher price. Today more subtle and carefully planned block busting is carried out by liberal and minority group organizations as a means to integrate the housing of a particular section.

The reactions of residents to the changes in ethnic composition have been marked by belligerent reactions, sometimes violent as well as legal and illegal means, to prevent a black or Puerto Rican from moving into their neighborhood. One well-known example of resistance regularly occurs when a black or Puerto Rican answers a rental ad in an Irish or Italian neighborhood. He is then told the apartment has been rented. As this is illegal in many areas, some landlords show only the least desirable apartments—that is, those with broken fixtures and peeling paint. The price of the rent may be raised and coupled with no commitment to improve the premises, the apartment hopefully becoming undesirable. The next prospective tenant of the "proper" ethnic background may be given a guaranteed commitment to put the rooms in order, plus often offered a lower rent. In more affluent areas, landlords simply do not rent or sell direct, but instead place the housing in the hands of real estate agents who are expected to screen prospective tenants or buyers before bringing them by. Thus the behavior that will be considered an intrusion depends on the relative differences of ethnicity and class.

Intrusion into a community may depend on life style as well. In a well-to-do urban neighborhood a black lawyer may not be totally undesirable to the residents, while a white hippy-looking type may appear as a threat to destroy the whole block. Similarly, drug addiction centers and halfway houses may be violently opposed by residents as the cause of bringing undesirables into the area. Older residents of the Haight-Ashbury district of San Francisco still claim that the neighborhood first began to decline when the first long-haired youths appeared. In Berkeley, California, long-time residents suggested that it was not the college youth who ruined Berkeley, but the hangers-on, the nonuniversity people who flocked to the university area as a region for drugs and the good life.

There are of course those intrusions made by residents themselves: a loud party late at night, a renter who leaves his window open and plays a hi-fi at high volume, teen-agers who congregate on doorsteps and make a racket. In some of the poorer areas the fire escapes, rooftops, and alleyways are the site of children's play, adolescent courtship, and adult gatherings. The noise as well as the congregations themselves may be considered intrusions by the neighbors. Boys who gather and smoke on a corner or a pair of lovers who neck in an entranceway may appear offensive to residents who must walk by them.

In cities like New York, entire neighborhoods have shifted in ethnic composition within a decade or two. Twenty years ago in the East Tremont section of the Bronx, peoples of European extraction predominated and the percentage of blacks and Puerto Ricans was minimal. Today one is hard put to find a non-Puerto Rican or nonblack resident in East Tremont. The changes are rapid and the pain resulting from increased migrations and resistance to migrations is suffered on all sides.

In the traditionally Italian community of Belmont in the Bronx, major ethnic shifts occurred in the 1960s and early 1970s. Belmont, approximately the size of many American urban neighborhoods, is a square mile or so in size. It is buffered somewhat by public buildings, automobile lots, etc., on the north. To the east lie the Bronx Zoo and Botanical Gardens. The western borders were partially protected by the presence of the "el," which ran in a north-south direction. To the south lies East Tremont, now a black and Puerto Rican neighborhood.

The southern and eastern borders of Belmont have gradually and reluctantly retracted as the Italians have fought to maintain a homogeneous ethnic community. For years 180th Street stood as a last-ditch southern border between Italians on the one side and Puerto Ricans and blacks on the other. But this border has also been breached and for some time the blocks north of 180th Street became known as a no-man's-land.

The New York City Planning Department has admitted on several occasions that its policy is to build on such frontiers. For example, if a school is built on a border, the idea is that it will have to be used by peoples of both ethnic groups and presumably they will settle their ethnic differences and enter into some sort of new communal agreement. Consequently, in this no-man's-land at the south end of Belmont a large public housing project was planned on the border. The Italians immediately feared the consequences, seeing the whole project as an intrusion. In concert, Italian and Irish contractors and workers of that portion of the Bronx engaged in all sorts of stalling tactics to prevent completion of the construction. It took, in fact, almost ten years to complete the project, and it was only then possible because a deal was reached in that 50 per cent of the housing would be reserved for Italian-Americans and 50 per cent would go to other peoples, presumably Puerto Ricans and blacks. However, the federal government stepped in.

Since the construction was a federally funded housing project, it could be occupied only by those who made less than $5,000 per year. This virtually precluded any Italian residents, or any other working-class residents for that matter. Only the poor and very poor would move in. The Italians cried out that they had been tricked and the area rapidly developed into a battleground between young Italians and blacks. At the height of violence roving bands of youths also carried out sorties across the borders into the more central regions of the enclaves. From the Italian standpoint, these intrusions meant destruction of a community. From the other side, Italian resistance and types of reactions demonstrated the racism rampant in America.

Whole towns and cities experience similar problems. Some cities like Newark or Detroit have shifted in ethnic composition from predominantly European-American cities to ones ethnically mixed, and now heavily black. Sometimes whole nations are disturbed by the massive migrations of foreigners.[6] The latter often take the form of military invasions. Spanish culture and society will always bear the influence of Moorish medieval invasion and occupation. The Roman conquest of England was a major event in the history of that island country. Characteristically, those whose turf is intruded upon picture the invaders as warlike militarists who seek conquest out of greed. This is not too far from the picture

painted by the North Vietnamese of the American presence in
South Vietnam.

In very few instances in human history is it possible to
characterize territorial invasions as due simply to the personalities or greedy motivations of the participants. Even when
this might be the case, circumstances and times change. A
country considered militaristic in one instance may in another
be asked to arbitrate a dispute. Canadians fought alongside
Americans against the Japanese and then against the North
Koreans, but were invited by all parties to be part of the truce
team when the French left Indochina. Peoples who were
pictured as aggressive in one era may be thought of as peaceful or passive in another. No more greedy image exists than
that of the Spanish conquistadors of the sixteenth century.
Today Spain has one of the lowest homicide rates in the
world and is pictured on tourist brochures as a country of
flamenco, farming villages, bullfights, and cave paintings. The
Israelites in biblical times were often militaristic when Israel
lay in that amorphous undivided region of the Near East.
Deprived of a state, the Jews for some two thousand years
were thought of by the Western world as passive nonaggres-
sive people. But with the modern state of Israel lying once
again in the Levant, the charges and countercharges, the intrusions and defensive actions hardly lead Westerners to think
of Israelis as passive.

We humans have a sense of territoriality that we employ in
our daily activities. And as we move about with other people
we customarily respect claims to certain increments of space
made by others and in return expect them to respect our
claims. Problems arise when claims are ambiguous or
disputed. In American cities, these problems frequently can
be linked to the attitudes, values, and cognitive codes that
mark ethnic and class differences. Living in a large city like
San Francisco or New York, we may think we all share the
same language and common behaviors. And to some extent
we do. But there is also a language, body language and body
spacing, that we are less aware of and more likely to maintain

through the generations. Being relatively unaware of gesticulation and distancing, we also may not recognize or acknowledge someone else's claim for privacy or not notice the defensive behaviors employed to protect that privacy.

Chapter 4
DEFENSE

Hostility among animals usually occurs when one animal of a species intrudes into the territory of another, for all animals, including humans, defend their turf against the intrusions of others. The initial reactions of the occupant are those of defense: the statement of violation and the threat to attack if this does not suffice. Until the work of ethologists began to prove otherwise, defense of a territory was associated with threats, mock attacks, and even in some instances the eruption of violence. Corresponding defense behaviors in man were thought of in terms of locked doors, aggressive behaviors, armed guards, and armies. But too much attention has been focused on the fascinating, the gnashing of teeth, threat, and assault. Considerably more subtle are the less active everyday behaviors of territorial defense that do not catch attention, but do have impact.

In most animals the point at which the defense begins marks the boundary of the territory.[1] For those animals without a clearly visible boundary, such as a fence, wall, or the bark bitten off trees, the defense behavior defines the perimeters of the territory. People, too, mark a boundary by a variety of behaviors that include backing up to maintain a fixed interpersonal distance, staring or glaring at the intruder, or verbally admonishing him. The farmer who glares from a distance at a weekend hiker who is about to cut through his potato field is not far removed from the baboon who displays his canines at another baboon who approaches too close to his mate.

People also use their arms and legs, as well as other parts of the body, to form a temporary barrier to block access to a space which they are claiming as a territory. It is not as if there is a visible line or built artifact to mark a perimeter. But if we share similar coding systems, we observe the signals of intent. A woman who averts her eyes and face slightly, show- ing only the back of her arm and shoulder and a portion of hair, maintains the privacy of her eye space and face from the intruding stare of a man. It is a defensive behavior. When four people who are talking turn the fronts of their bodies into the middle of the group, their backs, arms, and legs block access to the center of the group.

When codes are not shared in common or when ambiguity is present, then more active measures are adopted. When two people approach each other on a path, each will engage in polite, normal, expected common-sense behaviors to avoid a collision. In avoiding a collision they also maintain a territory between them.

In addition, they will glance at each other at a distance of ten feet or more, then look down and away and thereby avoid prolonged eye contact. In moving their bodies and their eyes out of the space between them, they mark an invisible line of separation. A territory has been defined. But all of us are also familiar with the little dance that people sometimes go through when passing strangers in a corridor or on a narrow sidewalk. Some behavior makes the event temporarily ambig- uous and the dance helps recalibrate the situation so that the participants may pass comfortably. Sometimes a smile or a voiced comment is also necessary. These polite overtones of recalibration are at the same time subtle active defensive be- haviors.

Let's return for a moment to Tom and his family at Marblehead Beach. As Tom's family grew in numbers with the arrival of newcomers, it broke up into several smaller clusters with each separated from the others. By arranging their bodies and controlling eye movements and voice levels, each cluster could maintain a small measure of its own privacy. The empty spaces between clusters were in fact buffer zones that helped define the integrity of each cluster vis-à-vis the other clusters. The size of the spaces resulted from the ethnic background of Tom's family as they assembled in open public places at the level of density afforded by the beach. This was also true for the family as a whole, which claimed a space that was farther removed from the other gatherings on the beach. Family members respected this territorial separation by avoiding regular eye contact with those outside the family gathering.

There appeared to be an invisible, but quite obviously a mentally coded, line separating the various family clusters on the beach. This sense of the situation was continuously reinforced, for as new arrivals would enlarge a particular cluster, other clusters would correspondingly give way, yielding a piece of turf that maintained the former distances between them. The beach that morning was uncrowded. Should large numbers of people have arrived, some more noticeable readjustments of the space between the various family gatherings would have been necessary. At this point more active defense behaviors, such as glares, refusals to move, verbal comments, and the like, would also have occurred.

The beach at Marblehead is an instance where many strangers assemble in the same unmarked public space. Some members of the group, especially the men, might stand on the periphery of their group in a particular type of posture often called the akimbo position—the legs are spread apart and both hands are placed on the hips so as to widen the body. This behavior can block vision into the inner group on the one hand and block physical access on the other. These men are like perimeter guards who in other situations would be replaced by security men or policemen standing at the borders of a public event. On occasions these perimeter guards draw lines with their toes in the sand or imaginary lines on the harder surfaces of concrete or wooden floors. This behavior is similar to senior males among baboons or wolves who patrol the perimeter of the group's territory. Each monitors the approach of strangers, watches the person until he is beyond the group, or sometimes blocks the potential invader's path and challenges his reason for being there.

In relatively open, crowded, and large public places such as the waiting room at a train station, the rights of privacy may be defended in various ways. A standing or seated position with head and eyes held down and body curled inward discourages contact and involvement. Many people in this instance add an additional dimension by occupying themselves in some activity such as reading, writing postcards, and the like. Anyone who does accost another in the waiting area must observe a ritual of behavior that provides a plausible reason for an intrusion: "May I have a match?" or "Do you have the time?" are offered in a slightly supplicating tone of voice, accompanied by a lowered head and avoiding prolonged eye contact. Such behavior can yield compliance with the request. Sufficient smiling and amiability in the tone of voice may also initiate conversation among strangers. Or those who are accosted may give only token response, thus being polite but at the same time defending a right of privacy: this token or temporary relinquishing of territory is usually marked by such behaviors as a voiced comment, "Yes?" "Pardon me?" or "What is it?" and a pulling of the body into an erect posture and staring at the intruder. Moreover, stating the time or handing over a box of matches becomes an act of token compliance, to be ended at that point if at the moment of compliance the accosted looks away and avoids eye contact. Defense of the space of privacy can be further stated by placing an arm across the body, crossing the legs, or turning away slightly.

If the intruder shows the behaviors of a panhandler, salesman, religious proselytizer, or prostitute, the individual accosted may refuse to acknowledge the intrusion totally. He could emphasize the closed posture by turning away, crossing arms and legs, and covering the face. If he already holds such a posture, he may exaggerate by obviously tightening the crossed arms and legs. If these kinesic behaviors do not dissuade the intruder, he may then move to another location, perhaps in the direction of an official, a ticket taker or gate guard, or nearer to a group of strangers.

Inside public territories such as a theater, people often try to defend the immediate area around them by engaging in a characteristic posture that forms a barrier preventing passage. The person projects a leg into the open space toward the aisle and sets his elbow on the armrest while leaning his head on the open palm. The hand partially covers the face, thereby avoiding any potential eye contact. The body posture, the side and back of the body facing the aisle block access. In an uncrowded situation this defensive behavior will normally reduce the possibility of anyone claiming adjacent seats. Should access be demanded, however, the seated person under normal circumstances would then be forced to yield, alter his posture, and permit the person to enter.

Blocking vision and physical access are defense behaviors that can be employed to achieve similar results in the home. The following example illustrates the extent to which the body can be used to achieve a desired result.

A husband and wife did not get along well. They rarely spoke to each other. She refused to cook for him and he refused to eat her cooking. Consequently, he had to prepare his own meals in the kitchen. One particular day while the wife was at work in the kitchen, she heard the door open and recognized her husband's arrival. At that moment she was standing near the stove completing the preparation of dinner for herself and the children. At the sound of the door closing, she put her left hand on her hip and used her right hand to continue stirring in a pot. A few minutes later the husband appeared at the doorway. At this point she placed both hands on her hips, thus discontinuing her work but widening her stance about the stove.

He said nothing, but proceeded to the refrigerator where he took out a number of items of food. He then approached the stove from her left. She had not turned to face him, so that he was presented with the back of her body. As he moved closer to the stove, she stepped to her left, blocking his access. He changed course trying to go around her, but she stepped to the right and again blocked his access. He stepped quickly to her left, whereupon she moved again. However, his movement was only a feint and he skirted around her right and successfully reached the stove, whereupon she angrily stalked out of the room.

Not all blocking behavior in the home takes on such extremes, but there are numerous other instances in which rather overt and hostile defense measures are employed. Children disturbing parents, younger siblings encroaching on older siblings, a husband unnecessarily remaining in the kitchen while his wife prepares the meal—all provide occasions for defense behaviors. Two children sitting on the couch playing a game may well treat the arrival of a third child as an intrusion, especially if the child is younger. They might defend their space by exhibitionistically refusing to pay any attention to the new arrival. They can easily do this by turning away, drawing an arm across the face, or crossing their arms or legs. If this defense behavior does not yield the intended result, one or both of the two children may verbally say to the third, "Go away," or "Leave us alone."

Two people seated in adjacent chairs or on a sofa and engaged in a private conversation may defend against intrusion of others into their group by using their bodies and furniture as barriers. Feet placed on a coffee table, leaning forward and placing an arm to the forefront of the conversational space, or bodies turned slightly inward and legs crossed to form a circle discourage interruption. Avoidance of eye contact and not shifting the posture also act as refusals to acknowledge the approach of a new arrival. Again, a glare coupled with a voiced comment escalates the defense against the more persistent intruder. Of course, in Western society older people and people of status generally have more rights to challenge a potential intruder and order him to depart. In contrast, younger people and people of less status frequently find themselves in the position of yielding by social necessity to the demands of a higher-status intruder.

The regulation of intrusion and actions of defense, then, are largely a lexical-kinesic matter in our society. Which behaviors will be employed and the character of the defense are directly interlinked with the behaviors exhibited by a new arrival approaching an occupied space. We've often watched children playing on the floor scream at, attack, or seek parental intervention at the approach of another sibling who directly cuts through the play area or threatens to take some play object. These more active, hostile, and sometimes violent behaviors probably occur at times of overt, active, and direct intrusion. The manner of approach, the posture used, and the activities of the eyes and voice distinguish direct intrusion from a request to share the space. When a sibling approaches a play group and smoothly joins in, his head will be slightly lowered, his eyes averted, and he will pause momentarily at an imaginary boundary on the edge of the play cluster. The children already occupying the space move in synchrony with the arrival's movement's and smoothly provide room for the child.

These rules also extend to other family members and to many other situations that occur in the home. A household member, for instance, can approach others who are seated without being challenged, provided he has usual rights to be there and provided there is a vacant chair available to him. Nevertheless, the ritual of dropping head and eyes just before taking the seat or momentarily pausing at the threshold gives recognition and deference to an existing territory, to an existing assemblage, and thereby further reduces the chances of resistance.

These behaviors remind us of the old question: when do two approaching dogs decide to fight or play? The answer, as Lorenz (1966) and other ethologists have stated, rests in the behaviors of the approach. A direct line of approach, coupled with raised hair on the back of the neck and a stiff tail, is a sign of war. A wiggling, zigzagging trot with bent tail displays another code that can lead immediately into play (Bateson, 1955).

Blocking access also occurs at the boundaries of the residence itself. In suburbia the marking of a distinct private territory is first made by clearly defining the boundaries with a fence, hedge, lawn, dogs, or other such markers. Convention prescribes that strangers and other nonhousehold members avoid trespassing on the property unless they have a purpose for entering. Even then, the intruder will find an additional defensive barrier, a door that is usually shut and locked. Passing over the barrier of the door requires an invitation and then the observance of the ritual of head and eye dipping as the threshold is crossed.

In the city the urban apartment building will mark the "outer" territory with walls and an entranceway. This initial barrier may be supplemented with doormen, in-house telephones, and other electronic monitoring equipment meant to restrict access through the entrance into the building itself. The apartment perimeter will also be marked by walls and doors. Doors in the inner city have locks and peepholes to observe who is across the threshold.

In the urban apartment the only direct intersection of the residence with the outside world is the telephone, doorway, at times the windows, if the apartment is on the lower floors, and fire escapes. In the poorer sections of the city, older residents are the most vulnerable to intrusion and often live in morbid fear of the outside world. They guard the apartment perimeter with fervor. Like their neighbors, they often have three *or* four safety locks on the doors as well as some other bar to prevent forced entry. If someone rings the doorbell or knocks on the apartment door, they will rarely open it, preferring instead to challenge the potential intruder by hollering through the door. (Most tenements do not have the luxury of a peephole.) The typical response is a voiced, "Go away! I don't want any." Occasionally they do not respond to the knocking at all, pretending to be not at home.

In the case of public housing, perimeter defense is severely limited by federal law, and many of the surveillance techniques open to the affluent apartment dweller are forbidden the resident in public housing. There are, of course, public housing police in some of the larger projects and many apartment-building residents have established volunteer and rotating watch systems at night. But the unlocked entranceway and the nonelectronic surveillance of corridors reduce the barriers available to residents of public housing. Security, then, is uppermost in everyone's thoughts. Their apartment becomes the sole safe location they can depend on. The halls, entranceways, and grounds of public housing are feared with due reason: lacking adequate defense, they become potential and real locations for intrusions.

In many American suburbs the contrast is striking. During the day there are few apparent mechanisms of defense, aside from the occasional family dog. Hedges, grass, or low-lying fences are barriers only if they are respected. Homeowners do occasionally take more active steps, such as to holler from a window at a trespassing child or to rush out and chase a stray dog out of the flower bed. Most of the people on a block in suburbia know one another and expect that there will be few intruders aside from service personnel during the daytime.

At night the picture of suburbia has drastically changed over the past few years. In the suburbs surrounding New York City the crime rate, especially burglaries, has soared. Lights are left on inside the house, frequently some throughout the night, and two or more porch and walkway lights, and newer brighter street lamps are now common. Doors and ground-floor windows are secured. Many homeowners have installed electronic burglar alarms. Some communities have their own local police. And some residents pay fees to private agencies who provide from a passing auto nonregular surveillance of the property.

Similar types of perimeter defense occur at much larger levels of territoriality. In one form or the other, neighborhoods, towns, cities, states, and nations mark and register the boundaries of their territories. Borders will be defended vigorously, in the courts through legal means and in the streets through some type of security force. No better example of territorial integrity develops than in those instances of jurisdictional disputes among separate but competing law-enforcement agencies, as witnessed in the feuding that occurred among security forces following the assassination of President John Kennedy.

The role of territorial perimeter guard has become an actual occupation similar in function and effect in about every country of the world. The names may vary from security guard to soldier, depending on whether the turf being defended is private or public, municipal or national. In the

United States alone we must recognize that those employed directly or indirectly in perimeter defense represent a staggering proportion of the population. If we include immigration officials, treasury agents, and national guardsmen and reserves with the regular military and police forces, the weight of perimeter defense becomes immense.

But these are the more visible elements of public and private defense. Just as people will use less apparent defense mechanisms when in public or at home, so will they do the same at the borders of neighborhoods and municipalities. In stable, homogeneous neighborhoods, residents scrutinize the passage of strangers very much as a *concièrge* monitors the movement of strangers into an apartment building. Residents who adopt a street-watching position do so by assuming a characteristic posture in a characteristic location near a window or doorway. In the doorway, for instance, they will usually lean against the outer wall and fold arms across chest.

Territorial defense also includes the structures that man builds. In the course of human evolution, people have devised ever more elaborate means of providing themselves with shelter. These become the physical artifacts of a creative genius, the concrete representations of varied needs for shelter, and the territorial markings of the beginnings and endings of a claimed piece of space. Among their other purposes, hedges, fences, walls, buildings, and compounds are physical extensions of human behavior. The house is a shelter, but it is also a behavioral representation of a particular territory. It is a built territory. The walls of a house define one type of defense, for they prevent the intrusions of vision, voice, and physical access. Once inside, more walls and doors defend against intrusion by separating rooms and even whole sections of the house. Within each room, furniture and room dividers block both vision and access and thereby order the movement and behaviors of people in the room.

Such territories fall into a pattern of three concentric zones of spaces: the nucleus, region, and "surround" (Scheflen with Ashcraft, 1975). The nuclear zone of a house consists of the living room, dining room, and in the older American and British houses the center hall. Guests will be invited into this

area. Around this zone of the house lie the kitchen, laundry
rooms, storage areas of the basement and attic, bedrooms and
other rooms ancillary to the sleeping portions, and in some
cases a front or rear porch. Still more peripherally lies the
yard, or third zone of the suburban and rural house. In
agrarian areas this "surround" may also include barnyards,
garden plots, and cultivated fields or pastures.

In the city this outer region of the "surround" almost
disappears. In the row house the yard is only a residual plot
of land maybe a square rod in size at the front and back of
the house. In the case of the apartment house, the entire "surround" of each apartment has disappeared or appears at best
in the communal areas of laundry rooms, corridors, elevators,
stairways, and lobbies. Larger apartment buildings, especially
some of the newer luxury high-rise affairs, sometimes set
aside a small open area at the front of the building for
grounds, fountains, scrubs, or a driveway, which can also be
classified in the "surround."

The apartment dweller has sacrificed the "surround" or has
relegated it to communal use; the region of the dwelling itself has also been markedly reduced in size. Only the rich can
afford a second story, which dramatically separates the sleeping portions. Utility spaces either disappear or are reduced to
a few square yards in the kitchen. The storage areas of basement and attic of the American house have given way to the
relentless need to make all available space more profitable.
Recreation rooms, patios, dens, and libraries, which form part
of the regional zone of even modest homes in suburbia, do
not remain in the apartment, except again in the most luxuri-
ous examples.

As the amount of total space decreases in the process of urbanization, the clarity of defensive boundaries among portions of the living quarters decreases also. Sleeping and entertaining areas will not be separated by a floor, or in many
apartments even by a corridor.

In the studio apartment they will exist side by side in the
same room, shifting in function as the activity of entertaining
gives way to the activity of sleeping. In many apartments a
simple archway and open doorway form the only structural

defense separating kitchen from living room. A door may be the sole barrier between living room and bedroom. In many modern apartments the living and dining areas have become one room.

In short, the walled lines within the apartment in America have diminished in the last hundred years. Similarly in modern suburban housing the traditional system of center halls with corridors has with few exceptions vanished. Split-level and ranch-style houses even begin to eliminate corridors in other portions of the house as well. Americans must now walk through a room in order to enter another and thus interrupt the activities occurring in that room. For instance, in many homes one must walk from the living room through the dining room to reach the kitchen. In households with a family or rumpus room it may be necessary to continue on through the kitchen to reach one's destination. In Britain, by contrast, the tradition of the center hall has continued. This type of separation permits a convenient defense of separate activities through architectural form.

But the issue of the separation of space in the home may be more complicated than simple architectural changes may imply. This whole question of separation of activities probably follows from a British-American middle-class tradition. In the suburban home, for instance, family members spend a great deal of the evening pursuing different activities in separate rooms. This kind of separation and regular use of the entire living space is also characteristic of black American families. Working-class Italians and Puerto Ricans, in contrast, disperse less and frequently limit occupation of the home to a single room where all family members congregate and pursue joint or separate activities. It is quite typical for Puerto Rican family members to spend an entire evening huddled together at close quarters watching television, conversing, or doing homework. What would be an intolerable intrusion of noise and people in one group, then, would be rather normal in another.

Separation is a feature of residential distribution as well. Until very recently, large sections of the United States could be defined by cultural heritage: there were the British-

Americans of New England, the Pennsylvania Dutch, the Scandinavians of Wisconsin, the Mexican-Americans of the Southwest, and many others. This sort of separation along class and ethnic lines also occurs in many American cities where neighborhood enclaves have formed, with residents defending the social or ethnic integrity of the community. Today, for example the boundary between the Italian-American community of Belmont in the Bronx and the adjacent black and Puerto Rican neighborhoods of East Tremont is defended almost as adjacent national borders are defended between hostile nation-states. We find similar examples in Boston, Detroit, and the suburban regions of Long Island. Children of one ethnic group who cut through the neighborhood of the opposing group do so at the risk of being ridiculed or even attacked. Street youth gangs organize tracts of neighborhoods, banding together for mutual defense and for control of subterritories, and occasionally like warring armies joining forces to invade the turf of opposing neighborhoods. Adults who pass through the neighborhood of a hostile ethnic group also risk mugging and attack, especially at night when the ethnic homogeneity of a neighborhood is often reclaimed. This kind of territorial defense is usually interpreted as the simple result of extreme and persistent poverty. We cannot condone crime in any disguise, but we suspect that beyond the motivations of individuals and environmental explanations crime and violence are intimately linked to attempts at territorial defense.

Yet adjoining neighborhoods of different ethnic composition do exist side by side in relative harmony. In many sections of Manhattan, on the south side of Chicago, and in other parts of the United States white ethnic and black ethnic peoples live in adjacent neighborhoods and enjoy amiable relationships. Members of one group do not attack members of the other group and rarely accost one another. Much has been made of the high crime rates on the Upper West Side of Manhattan. But blacks, Puerto Ricans, Italians, Jews, and other white ethnics of working-class and middle-class backgrounds live in adjacent neighborhoods, even in some cases in adjacent blocks. During the daytime and early evening hours one cannot help but notice the superficially congenial relations of the mixed class and ethnicity of this section of Manhattan. People greet, nod, smile, and even converse in shops and on the streets. At night certain blocks do become extremely dangerous. However, recent newspaper reports of crime rates indicate that the supposedly safe and affluent Upper East Side runs a very close second in comparison.

It is easy to focus on certain events, especially those that occurred in Boston in 1975, and claim that cross-ethnic hostility hasn't really diminished. But in comparision with events that took place earlier in this century, changes have occurred. In the 1920s and 1930s, neighborhoods were much more segregated by ethnicity and social class. Members of a minority group appearing in a white middle-class neighborhood clearly gave evidence for being there and walked and moved with propriety. They exhibited a number of postural and kinesic conventions, such as a lowered head, moving out of the paths of strolling residents, etc. We observed the continuance of some of these behaviors by blacks who had to pass through the Italian community of Belmont in the Bronx. But then again Belmont is a community launched as a last-ditch stand to preserve an ethnic enclave. In other places, such as the wealthy Delancey Street area of Philadelphia, where blacks must pass on their way to public transportation, they do not comport themselves as if passing through hostile territory. They also frequently stroll, visit local restaurants, and congregate in Rittenhouse Square on weekends and early evening. With some exceptions, then, there is generally more freedom of movement and passage in America. These changes refer to people's movements through territories. Changes in residential distribution would be another matter.

Many regions of America maintain their separateness. Parts of the Deep South still display antipathy toward outsiders. Old New England Yankees differ little, and hill people of the Ozarks continue to be suspicious of outsiders. The territorial defense of nations also varies greatly along lines of ethnicity and social and economic considerations. The United States and Canada only perfunctorily defend their borders, but the United States is active in its defense along the border with

Mexico. White-controlled Rhodesia employs an active military defense of its borders with black African states. The borders between West Germany and Austria, both German-speaking countries, are little more than symbols of national identity, while the borders separating West Germany from East Germany or Northern Ireland and the Republic of Ireland are buttressed by armed military force.

When a perimeter between two ethnic, national, or social groups is clearly marked by visible boundaries and when the peoples involved are familiar with the system of marking boundaries, there is little room for ambiguity. It will be clear to all concerned exactly where the boundaries begin, exactly when they are crossing a boundary and how they must behave in doing so, and what to expect on the other side. However, if territorial boundaries are not clearly marked or if people do not share the same system of marking and observing boundaries, then ambiguities can develop. It is not just that someone will misinterpret but that he will also fail to recognize the existence of a border. Even though the person may not be intending an intrusion, the other side may perceive his behavior as such and take defensive action. A great deal of the violence and unpleasantness of our present social existence may be due simply to ambiguities in coding of territories.

Some ethnic groups of America are openly friendly and amiable with strangers when they meet on neutral grounds. Peoples of Eastern European Jewish descent as well as some inhabitants of Western America will approach with little hesitation and strike up conversations with other Americans or English-speaking peoples if they should meet in a neutral public place like Rome, Paris, or London. Many of the traditional Yankees and the British do not do this and feel accosted when approached, considering this behavior forward and aggressive. They may respond to the intrusion in curt, sometimes rough terms and proceed to ignore the intruder. In turn, those who do not follow such friendly congenial behaviors when on neutral turf are labeled haughty, cold, reserved, snobbish, or just plain unneighborly.

These types of misunderstandings occur more frequently

when the customs of interaction differ. Variations in the use of the eyes, interpersonal distancing, and touching can quickly lead to misunderstandings and defensive behaviors. For instance, Cubans and Puerto Ricans, who stand at very close distances by British-American, black American, and Northern European standards, are frequently perceived as pushy, impolite, or sexy, depending on the adjective chosen by the accuser.

Joseph English reports that many Americans who served in the Peace Corps in Latin America were rather continuously in heterosexual and homosexual panic. Ashcraft has often discussed the different cultural conventions of dress, eye behavior, and attitudes about sex in the Caribbean with local Peace Corps volunteers, but they were still observed to interpret the same behaviors according to their own coding system. In one country three female volunteers organized a two-week summer camp in the countryside for middle-class urban teen-age girls. The girls were in their early teens and clearly delighted to get away from the scrutiny of family and friends in the city. The local teen-age boys were also delighted at this "gift from heaven." However, to everybody's chagrin, the Peace Corps women ran close herd on their charges, refusing to allow any fraternizing with the local males. By the end of the camp, the volunteers had managed to antagonize just about all concerned. One volunteer replied to a charge that they had acted a bit overzealously because, given the openly aggressive behaviors of both the local boys and girls, it was necessary to put a protective wrap around them to prevent any disaster. These behaviors, interpreted by a middle-class American woman as "openly aggressive," are to anyone raised in the Caribbean no more meaningful than those behaviors that would be exhibited between American boys and girls. In this instance, then, middle-class American values dictated two weeks of activities in a Caribbean country where both attitudes and behaviors of adolescents differed markedly from those who organized the trip.

Problems also arise when attitudes vary toward the use of public spaces. In some of the older and more traditional residential neighborhoods of a city, residents consider the parking spaces in front of their houses reserved for local inhabitants and resent those who treat the blocks as any other urban public street. Chairs, beach baskets, and the like are sometimes used to reserve parking spaces. Others who drive in from outside the neighborhood, not recognizing any reason why they should avoid these areas, proceed to park there. Similarly the typical urban dweller accustomed to the catch-as-catch-can of public street parking carries this value to suburbia. He soon finds that in suburbia it is an intrusion to park in front of someone's house unless the visit is being made to that person, to the person next door, or the person across the street. In Garden City, an affluent suburb of New York, we've watched residents walk out and ask visitors not to park on the street in front of their houses.

An analogous situation occurs in the public parks of a city. If a park is located in a particular ethnic neighborhood, for instance, the residents around the park will consider that they and their neighbors from the immediate surroundings have exclusive rights to the use of the park. They view the use by peoples of other ethnic or social and economic groups as an intrusion, an invasion of their space. Overt monitoring, glares, and the like may accompany the appearance of an outsider.

In contrast, Central Park in New York and Golden Gate Park in San Francisco are used rather freely by all social classes and ethnic groups, and local residents seem to lay no special claim to the park. Residents who live nearby may complain about the littering, the "types" who enter the park, the park's invasion by other riffraff, and how unsafe it is. But these parks are not considered neighborhood parks by authorities, local residents, or the public at large. They become a kind of universal urban public turf. Moreover, their size may also play a role in the lack of any significant claim.

Most private properties in the city are clearly marked, and any intruder knows well that he has crossed a border. But Oscar Newman (1972) and others have shown that many public housing projects have no visible or distinguishable borders. Federal law does not permit the blocking or fencing off of a project from the surrounding neighborhood. Consequently, as Newman demonstrates, everyone treats the project as open territory. In turn, the residents of a project after repeated unsuccessful attempts to defend the unmarked borders simply gave up. As the population per floor and per apartment house increases, surveillance and responsibility for entranceways, open spaces, and corridors decrease. In turn, vandalism and crime at these locations increase (Newman, 1972).

The defense of a territory is more automatic and marked by less violence when the borders are clearly visible and understood by all and when the population of the area is relatively homogeneous.

Chapter 5
CONSTRAINTS

As frightening as it may seem to some, there is no unbounded space left. Even when the great cattle barons of the old West laid out huge tracts of land that no fence could possibly mark, they did not simply move in and occupy an unclaimed territory. At first the early Westerners lived in relatively peaceful association with the indigenous American Indians of the Southwest. Each used the land differently and the sparse population reduced the frequency of conflict. As the cattle herds grew in size, and the population expanded in concert with economic opportunities, and the general affluence of the country brought the railroads to the West, conflicts over territory increased to the point where one population nearly annihilated another.

Today we are more certain of where our borders lie. No longer do we brazenly speak of open lands to be had by those who are willing to settle them. We must comport ourselves, to some extent anyway, within the framework of the laws of a national entity, and this holds even for the most remote of regions. This is true as well for the not so obvious territories that are defined by simple body movements and postures and by the layout and construction of houses, apartment complexes, and office buildings. Acts of privacy, rules against intrusion, and the behaviors of defense do not occur as shreds and patches, but instead are systematically organized to define boundaries and enclose space.

Let us examine in some detail the small and temporary spaces that people enclose with their faces, gazes, and the orientation of their bodies, since both the physical occupation of a given space and the direction or orientation of the human body define and claim a given territory.

Returning to the early moments of the scene at Marblehead Beach, we will recall that Tom sat alone on the sand looking off at the water and beach line. With just the movement of his head and eyes he could scan a large section of beach area. Within his frame of vision lay a territory that he claimed with his eyes and orientation of his body. To be sure, this was a rather vague and loosely structured territory and people passing along the beach in his field of vision would not consciously think they were violating someone's private space. Yet to some degree they did treat this space as a territory. As they would walk through the area framed by the front of Tom's body and vision, they averted their eyes and usually lowered their heads, especially if they were near him. Similarly a row of people watching a distant event look in the same direction. They collectively *share a* space. A theater audience watches the performance on stage and their view, or the "space" between performers and audience, is respected.

A more definitive space developed when Tom and the couple began talking. In facing one another, the threesome marked off an inner conversational space that they would more readily defend and expect others to respect than the less evident space Tom had claimed while sitting and facing the ocean. Anyone would have felt uneasy about staring into their inner area.

This inner space was formed by the manner in which the threesome focused the front of their bodies and their faces and eyes. When they were joined by the young man, they expanded the size of this inner area, but the general orientation of their bodies remained the same and the inner space continued to be respected. It would remain so for the duration of the conversation, fading out as the members took other positions when the family assembly enlarged. This inner space (technically an orientation space) was a yard to a yard and a half in diameter. But the total space claimed by the participants was larger, as it also included the space occupied by their bodies.

However, if the activity occurred in a theater in the round or in an oval stadium, many rings of spectators would surround the center field or stage and collectively they would be oriented toward the performance from all directions. The space in this case would be circular or oval in shape. Therefore, when humans build or wall in a space, the resulting configurations will probably be rectangular, circular, or oval. In fact, since the beginnings of agriculture, what archaeologists call the neolithic, patterns have changed from round- or oval-built spaces to square or rectangular ones; and since at least Egyptian and Mayan times, there has been a further favoring of rectangular shapes at the expense of square ones. We do not understand why the preferences for the various shapes have occurred, however.

The conventional shapes that humans use when designing a building or other structure, then, are based on the spaces that are formed by the direction in which the human body faces. These spaces of orientation build from the simple single direction of Tom facing the ocean to a more complex multidirection that occurs when a row, column, or circle of people face a common focus. Unit-by-unit orientation spaces combine to increase the total space much the same as the letters of the alphabet combine, forming words, and words combine to form sentences and paragraphs in the structure of a language. But just as words are not simply combinations of letters, so is orientational space not described simply by adding the orientations of all present.

If a gathering of people assemble for a beach party, picnic, or cocktail party, there will not be a single orientation nor a single rectangle or circle of mutual orientations. Instead there will be several orientations, as many clusters of people face one another within their own particular little cluster. People or groups of people move through the gathering at large,

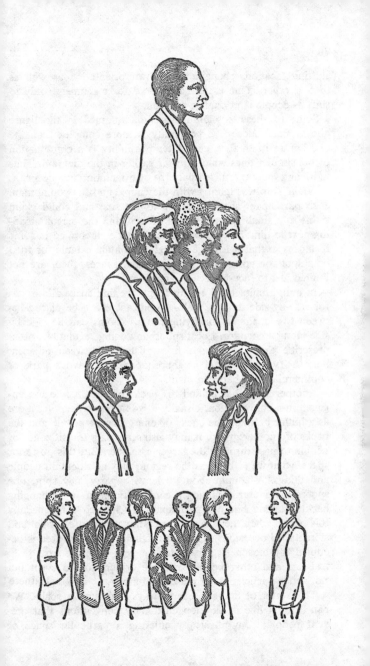

shifting location, changing their own orientation as well as that of others. One pattern may hold for a moment, only to shift as people later change position.

Some of these possibilities are diagrammed in the figure above. Each successive possibility is more complex than the one before it. In fact, each later possibility is a combination of the simpler ones which appear earlier in the diagram. Thus more and more organized patterns of orientation can occur.

When Tom was talking with the couple and the young man, each participant shared a space to the side and could claim rights to a small space between himself and the person standing next to him. Side-by-side space may be elaborated in some instances so that it is large enough to contain a table for food or a spot for possessions. Interpersonal spaces, then, are not limited just to face-to-face arrangements.

In built architectural arrangements we find space allotments for side-by-side units as well. An end table can be placed between two chairs in the living room. Rooms can lie side by side along a corridor. Local suburban zoning regulations often prescribe that there be a fixed distance between adjacent houses. Two residential neighborhoods may have a park or commercial strip between them.

Another space lies behind the backs of people who are engaged in a conversation. Usually it is left empty, serving more as a buffer between the backs of one group of people and the backs of another group. It may also serve as a transit zone for people to pass through the larger assembly. But this posterior space, what we refer to as the region, may also contain people and things. A couple about to leave a party may split, one spouse momentarily joining a conversation, the other hanging back, listening but not participating. Children often occupy this region when their parents are talking. In more formal and stereotyped occasions such as a football game, this area is occupied by coaches, substitutes, judges, timekeepers, team trainers, and other people who are critical to the event but not active participants in the central arena.

There are, of course, several ways to bound a space. We can draw a line or develop customary conventions that prevent people from physically entering a particular space or crossing through it. The sideline markers of a football field are effective barriers to some personnel during the course of the performance. Coaches, managers, other members of the team may cross that line only with special permission, and in some instances certain people may never enter the playing field. There is the strict taboo, for instance, against the coach crossing the line to enter the playing field under any condition. Similarly we customarily respect a funeral ceremony by not crossing the imaginary boundary which separates the members of the funeral entourage from any spectators who may pause at or pass by the event. Parishioners do not step up or cross into the altar area during church ceremonies. But while these borders prevent physical access to the space, people can look into it and across it and sometimes interact with those occupying the space. A coach hollers commands onto the field; the congregation enters into a ritualized response to the priest saying the Mass.

A second type of boundary is that of the low barrier, which, like the line, restricts physical access but does not prevent others looking into or speaking into the territory. The police barrier of wooden sawhorses, the iron railings of grandstands, the railing around the orchestra in a theater, furniture arrangements in the living room are examples of low barriers used to subdivide territories and mark off certain spaces. Finally, a third way to bound space is the wall that totally blocks off the space from physical access, vision, and to some extent sound.

Architects and interior designers have employed combinations of these principles in order to construct various divisions of interior space. Generally, however, their plans fall into one of two types of patterns: first, a space is divided at the two ends, giving a head and foot appearance, or along the two sides, or into a combination of head, foot, and sides. In the modern urban apartment, for instance, a large room is frequently divided so that one section becomes a kitchen-dining area and the other a living room. In an office building a rectangular-shaped space may be divided by constructing a corridor down the middle and erecting offices on either side.

Some theaters are divided with a central portion of orchestra seats at one end and a stage at the other. Another set of spectator seats runs along each side.

Secondly, spatial division falls into a pattern of concentric zones with a central zone or nucleus surrounded by other zones. In the dining room, a table and chairs define the central area, while a combination of sofa, chairs, and coffee table accomplish the same in the living room. Surrounding this nucleus is a region for other furniture, such as a buffet and extra chairs in the dining room and plants, hi-fi set, and bookcases in the living room. This arrangement of concentric zones that divide and redivide space is common to all levels of territorial organization, from a room to a city, town, or state. One feature of this system is that the various zones can be divided so that any enclosed space can be subdivided to form as many as six concentric zones. For instance, the central area of the dining-room table and chairs can be further divided into an inner zone of the table and its contents and an outer zone of chairs and the people who sit there. The outer, or regional, zone, such as the spectators' area in a stadium, can also be divided into a seating section, a ticket and refreshment section, and an exterior parking zone. A city may be organized with a nuclear zone of public and commercial buildings, a region of residential blocks and neighborhoods, and a wider surrounding zone of industrial parks or open spaces. The city of Paris was *originally* designed in this pattern. It is also possible for cities to have multiple nuclei, as is the case in New York. In Manhattan there is a central zone for shopping called Midtown, a central zone for commercial activity, Downtown, and a central zone for entertainment, Broadway.

What this way of looking at human space accomplishes is that it permits us to see space as a system of interrelated and interdependent territories. Einstein broke the ground for this approach: he did not accept the notion prevalent in his day that one planet acted on another planet, a sort of billiard ball theory that Newton had postulated. Instead, he pictured the pattern of motion among planets as a function of a large "field" he described as the interdependency of speed and mass. Interplanetary bodies move in ordered ways. So does human behavior and so does the arrangement of human space.

A system, or "field" of human space forces us to recognize that human territories are not simply comprised of a series of discrete and separate spaces, like ten separate houses on a block, but, instead, that any particular space is also a very integral part of a larger system of spaces, those ten houses arranged in a very definite pattern linking each house to the others on the block. To recognize the obvious fact that a room lies within a house and a house within a neighborhood becomes an important step in understanding how spaces are used, how they are lived in.

Thus a chair occupies one location among several other locations in a room. The chair may form part of a dining-room cluster and its particular location is interdependent with the locations of other occupied spaces in the cluster, such as the chairs that surround a dining table. The "field" in this case is the configuration of the cluster. The room layout has a nucleus containing tables and chairs and a region for storage and passage. The room itself, however, is also a single location among others in the house. The immediate "field" of the room, then, is the arrangement of room layouts in the dwelling. The house, in turn, also has a nucleus consisting of interconnecting rooms such as the kitchen and living and dining rooms and a region consisting of bedrooms, baths, work spaces, and storage areas. The house occupies a particular space within a larger more inclusive area of the neighborhood, and the immediate "field" of the house is the arrangement of houses in the neighborhood. Neighborhoods are part of a city, town, or county.

We have thus built from the space occupied by a single chair to a much larger spatial increment. Within an Einsteinian framework, each particular arrangement lies within a larger more encompassing arrangement, which in turn lies within an even larger more encompassing arrangement: "fields" lie within "fields" (see Appendix A).

Should a person cast his eyes from his location to another, his gaze will cross a boundary of some kind. And if he walks from his location to another, he crosses a boundary, too. In fact, as one moves from place to place, one crosses a multitude of boundaries at all levels of organization. *And each crossing requires some recognition of the conventions of passage.* Each border crossing is gated, that is, a border is open to some people on some occasions for some purposes and it is closed to some people on some occasions for some purposes. This can include the simple behaviors of eye movement and gaze direction, or movement through the rooms of a house, or crossing into certain neighborhoods, or crossing national borders. All such situations are gated, and to violate the rules of crossing, either wittingly or unwittingly, is to invade a privacy or create an intrusion.

Crossing from one territory to another, one enters into a new jurisdiction. Some other person, group, or institution has power there and establishes or tries to establish rules or laws about what can occur and how any action should be carried out. In addition, each territory lies under some aegis, that is, under some system of conventional local, class, or ethnic customs. Those who enter are expected to know or learn to know the differences in constraints put upon their behavior in one territory after the other.

The matter is even more complicated, for any particular territory will lie within a hierarchy of jurisdictions and customs. Since a territory may lie in a room, in a house, in a neighborhood, in a town or city, in a state, and in a nation, rules and laws at each of these levels more or less apply. We are not accustomed to thinking of this multiple influence, but we so comport ourselves in any daily heterogeneous situation. Thus, for instance, in New York, a person may occupy a location in a household governed by Jewish-American customs, but live within a predominantly black American neighborhood that lies in a borough governed by Italian-American politicians, that in turn lies under the jurisdiction of a largely British-American state.

But it is not simply that different rules govern each territorial crossing and occupation. It is also that some people cannot cast their eyes into certain spaces at all and that some people cannot enter certain territories except on the most unusual of occasions. Actually few people, if any, have an un-limited range of movement. All of us are restricted to a rela-tively few locations in the larger social order.

With a great deal of hesitation due to the impact of outside influences and variations, it is possible to describe the tradi-tional amounts of space characteristic of the middle-class British-American heritage. The British-American middle class is an appropriate illustration because peoples from this back-ground were principally responsible for building America. It is on their blueprints and their traditional space sizes that the country has been erected with buildings and other space layouts. Those people coming from other traditions to this country have had to live in British-American space, whether they have liked it or not. Only very recently have Danish or Mediterranean furniture and Italian and Spanish room and house layouts played any significant role in American space. There are, of course, the exceptions in certain sections of the country such as New Orleans, California, and the Southwest, where Spanish and French architectural styles prevailed. Even in many of these areas, though, the extent of "progress" has been to impose a standardized tradition on architecture, a tradition which dates back to a long history of British-American culture.

A basic increment of space in the British-American tradi-tion is approximately two cubic yards in size. Its ground or floor area is a square yard. This is the characteristic distance that an adult British-American maintains during conversation in an uncrowded setting. Since the size of the human body is approximately one quarter of two cubic yards, the space size permits its occupant to gesticulate, hold possessions and chil-dren, shift from one leg to the other, step forward to be closer to another conversationalist or backward to maximize space, or move laterally to be closer or farther away on each side.

If three people are together talking, their position will shift during the course of the conversation. The distances between them will vary according to culture, the situation, and inti-macy of the conversation. Here is an example of what might happen during five minutes of conversation:

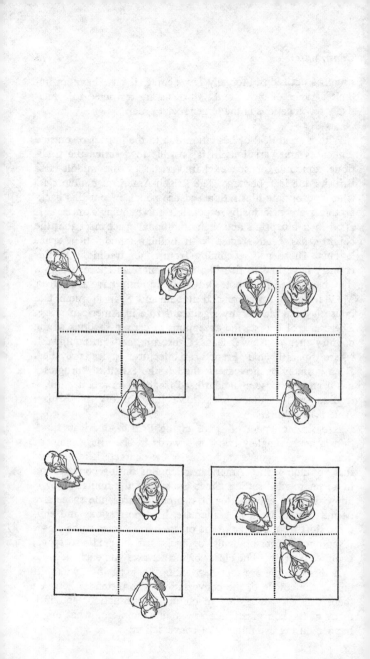

This size, approximately two square yards, happens also to be built into British-American furniture. The full-sized living-room chair and the seat in first class on airplanes and Pullman cars are about this size. The seat itself is some 18 inches wide and 21 inches deep. It has leg-room space in front of 18 or more inches. Each armrest is at least 3 inches wide. Thus the chair space in British-American furniture approximates 24 inches wide by 54 inches deep.

The size of the British-American area itself is 30 square yards, or 272 square feet. This is an increment of space equivalent to one square rod. (Since the eleventh century the British rod has been standardized at 16.5 feet.) In domestic space the dimensions of a room have been gradually rectangularized at 15 by 18 British feet, or 5 by 6 yards. This size room can be traced to the ninth-century Saxon dwelling and is found in the more successful working-class and middle-class homes in England. With few exceptions it served as the model for American architectural construction. The living room, dining room, kitchen, and master bedroom are this size in the old New York brownstone, the Baltimore and Philadelphia row house, colonial Connecticut house (in the colonial house both bedrooms upstairs were each a square rod, thus duplicating in space the parlor and hall below), and most middle-class suburban and rural homes in the Northeast until about 1920.

The rod-sized room is, however, of much more ancient and diversified origins. Rooms of this magnitude are found in domestic dwellings in Egypt and Greece. It appears as the size of the stoa in ancient Athens. It occurs in the base and divisions of the Roman basilica, the Carolingian, Romanesque, and Gothic cathedrals. A room of this size even appears in early Mayan and pre-Aztec cultures in the Valley of Mexico around 11 A.D. The size is not used for less important rooms, such as bathrooms, storage rooms, work areas, and children's bedrooms of nineteenth- and twentieth-century houses in America. These rooms are smaller in size. In the contemporary American house we will discover that even the main rooms have shrunk to less than a square rod in size.

A distance of 4 linear rods is equal to 66 feet, the length of

the British surveyor's chain. This unit also forms an important measurement running through British-American history.
It has served as a common base increment for the size of
urban lots, street widths, and other built territories. Again, 66
feet forms part of a traditional unit measure that can be
traced to ancient Egypt. It also appears in pre-Aztec and
Mayan cultures. The Street of the Dead at Teotihuacán, for
instance, is 66 feet wide. Since four bays of a rod each consti-
tute the width of European cathedrals, the interior width is
commonly 66 feet in England, northern France, and Germany. By the same token, the wide streets of Manhattan,
Philadelphia, and other northeastern cities are 66 feet wide.

The characteristic length of the urban lot in the older
northeastern cities is based on an increment of the rod and
chain. Thus they are almost universally 8 rods, or 2 chains
deep. However, the front and rear rod of these properties
have been surrendered to the public domain for streets and
alleyways. This leaves the owner with a realistic depth of 99
feet, or 6 rods. The width of a block in Manhattan is 4
chains, or about 198 feet, and the length is 16 chains. This
yields a 1-to-4 ratio for the city block. In old central Philadelphia, however, the blocks are square, being 4-by-4 chains.
City blocks in Chicago are on a 1-to-3 ratio, or 1½ chains
by 4½ chains. Whatever the ratio, the common denominator
is a measurement based on increments of the British rod
and chain.

Another traditional British measure influencing American
culture is the section, a unit equaling one square mile. The
Old City of London was this size. Many traditional urban
neighborhoods in American cities were also one square mile.
For instance, old central Philadelphia lies between four
main streets, with the central area and the city hall in the
middle and a small park at each corner. Each of the four
sections is one square mile. Agricultural land in the United
States was also measured in sections, but the sections were
then subdivided by acres. Thus most of the land grants and
early sales to immigrants were a section, or 640 acres, or one
square mile in size. At other times in American history a subdivision of the section, such as a quarter or an eighth of a

section, was used as a basis for land sales. These subdivisions gave the landholder an area that could be measured in acres. Thus, for instance, at the end of the Civil War, Union soldiers were offered land at an allotted 40 acres and a mule.

These traditional measurements, the rod, chain, and mile, are not just historical curios. They become significant in other ways because they are increments of space used as a basis for laying out homes, lots, city blocks, neighborhoods, and towns and cities since the beginnings of American settlement. They date even into early English history. It is always surprising to hear population experts and city planners discuss problems of the city using acres as a model. The acre is a measurement of rural, not urban land. Why population densities and architectural features are not described according to the measures used to construct a space layout is simply beyond comprehension. On a 10-times basis the acre does become an interesting measure, but why not refer to rods or miles as they were originally laid out? How can we use a base 10 measure when housing space, and much of the urban land space, in Britain and America is laid out on a base 2 or base 4 system of increments? For example, there are 4 rods to a chain, and often 4 chains to a block.

It is only in the last century that a decimal system has become commonplace in American building habits and land surveying methods. The engineer's chain is 100 feet and is likely to be used now as a means of subdividing properties. It should become an interesting game for architects concerned with restoration of early Americana. If all new measurements will be made within the metric system or a system of tens, or hundreds, then what does the architect do with a house built in 1740? Similarly, land in England, Northern Europe, and the United States has usually been laid out in multiples of 4, 16, 64, etc., very similar to the system employed by the Greeks of 4 dactyls to the palm and 4 palms to the cubit. Southern European lands tend to follow the Roman or decimal pattern of 10, 50, 100, etc.

In any event, American housing is now built on a mixed system combining a base 10, or decimal system with a base 2, which, of course, all adds to the complexity of trying to understand pattern in human space. It may take some time to get Americans familiar with a foot, yard, rod, chain measurement system, a system found in the interpersonal distances of interaction, to become familiar with and adjust to a metric system which will yield quite different increments of space and interpersonal space units. Those who believe it is possible to borrow a unit from another culture without picking up a much larger package simply don't understand the complexity of culture and the interconnectedness of the parts.

Having described traditional increments of space, we can within limits also describe any changes and distortions in the size of a piece of land, room, or house by matching them against traditional British-American standards. In this sense, we may possibly be able to discuss differences in space allocation. Without doubt, the wealthy and higher social classes will claim larger increments than the urban poor. More importantly, in talking about space gain or loss, we can become aware of any trend in the population at large which increases or decreases these traditional allocations.

A space decrement in America began around 1920, or approximately at the time this country changed its immigration laws and closed its doors to all but the selected. Not only has peripheral or regional space been lost in the urban apartment but the size of the space per se has diminished. Even suburban homes have living rooms, dining rooms, and kitchens less than a square rod in size. In city apartments and lower middle-class housing the living room, for instance, is closer to 10 by 14 feet. This compares to the traditional rectangular rod-sized room of 15 by 18 feet. In the ghetto apartment the space is even smaller. Urban housing in New York City, especially the old tenements, were built for a working-class population. Today in the black and Puerto Rican ghettos of the Bronx, these same units have been divided and subdivided, decreasing their complete size significantly from the period of the 1920s. The average ghetto apartment now has only about 2 square rods in total space.

The living area of the luxury New York urban apartment has remained about one square rod, but it is now more rectangularized, shifting from a 15-by-18 footage to a 14-by-19 footage. But this area no longer is simply a living room. It has in fact become in many instances a condensation of two rooms in which a dining area takes up approximately a third of a square rod, leaving two thirds remaining for the living room. This is an absolute loss of the one full square rod from the pre-1920 period. We would find a similar picture comparing older middle-class suburban and rural housing with contemporary middle-class suburban housing.

The process of urbanization yields continued condensation: multiple units are placed in the same dwelling, and multiple dwellings are placed within the same building. That is, what would occupy more than one housing unit and outside space for rural America becomes combined internally within the housing unit of the urbanite. Then the unit itself is made into a multiple dwelling by stacking "homes" on top of one another. In addition, there is a progressive loss of the various regions of the house itself. The apartment dweller has no basement or attic for storage, and it is rare to find an apartment with a second floor so that sleeping areas are less separated from living, entertaining, and dining areas. Traditional spaces such as the pantry disappear or remain at best as a small closet or corner shelf space. Kitchens practically cease as separate rooms or remain as 4-by-6 corner spaces that may be enclosed on three sides but open into the living-dining area. Living and dining areas coexist in the same room. Hallways disappear. And bedrooms become much smaller.

There is another issue, and this is the question of what is sufficient space. A widowed person living alone in a large suburban house may have more than enough room. But two warring marital partners occupying a space similar in size may complain bitterly of a lack of room. A century ago only a handful of mountain people roamed through the state of Colorado. The city of Denver was hardly overpopulated. Today sufficient room in Denver is becoming a critical problem, and ranchers in the outlying regions complain about the influx of tourists, industry, and masses of people from the East and West Coasts.

There is much more to this issue of sufficient space than

just numbers of people. For example, the amount of room
varies also with the activity. An area possibly 30 square yards
in size will be quite sufficient for eight to ten people sitting
quietly and engaging in conversation. But this same space
would be totally inadequate for them to play a game of bad-
minton. Similarly a few city blocks can give residence to hundreds of people and a number of shops. A hundred acres,
however, is quite inadequate in contemporary America for
even small and limited farming operations.

At one time great herds of buffalo wandered across the
American plains, moving slowly with the seasons from one
pasture to the other. Following the buffalo were the Indian
tribes of the Great Plains. To what extent the Indian hunted
buffalo prior to Cortez's sweep into Mexico is still a debated
issue. One thing that is apparent, though, is that the introduction of the horse into the New World by the Spanish
significantly shifted Plains Indian culture in the seventeenth
and eighteenth centuries. Space sufficient for people migrating
on foot proved to be no longer adequate for a community
moving on horseback. The need for larger territories significantly altered social organization and increased inter-
tribal contact. To some extent the warfaring practices of the
Plains Indians, so romanticized in American popular media,
probably were due in large part to the horse and the consequent need for larger territories.

Rural peoples are accustomed to large increments of space.
Long-time urban residents, in contrast, have developed a life
style more appropriate to the metropolitan density and size
of buildings and rooms. Stan Jones (1969) argues that even
the traditional ethnic interpersonal differences disappear in
the crowded public places of New York City. Nevertheless,
immigrants from rural states such as South Carolina or Utah
find the spacing in New York oppressive, while children
raised in the ghettos of New York frequently feel extremely
uncomfortable when taken for outings in the country. We
have seen these children either huddling together with little or
no mobility or running wildly and frantically through the
available space.

The problem of sufficient space is compounded by how

each person feels about space. Some people always stand close and touch regardless of their background. Many die-hard urbanites hate elevators, feeling claustrophobic as soon as they enter one with more than one or two people. Architects and planners face this problem continuously. There simply is no space that they can design which will please all who occupy it. To make matters more complicated, attitudes toward space may be symbolic. A person may feel claustrophobic not as a result of the size of the space but because of who is in it. There are many white Americans who "feel" uncomfortable in a huge waiting room of a hospital or railroad station if a black American is also present. The more blacks present, the more the person feels confined within a cramped space. In short, many human values and experiences aside from size of the space contribute to satisfaction.

Whether we have enough space is a political question.[1] Any answers that may be forthcoming must take into account the age-old problems of uneven distribution of wealth and the consequences in terms of who gets what, where, when, and how much. Spatial increments also vary as we move from one cultural tradition to another. Thus the British have traditionally laid out tracts of land and erected buildings on them according to one set of spatial values, while Mediterranean peoples have divided space by other standards. What would be considered a "normal," or traditional increment of space is bound to class and culture.

Chapter 6
CROWDING

Crowding is an unpleasant subjective experience, but at the same time we know very little about its consequences for man.

History records the story of the Black Hole of Calcutta. In 1756 Fort William, the British settlement in Calcutta, was captured by Siraj-ud-daula. One hundred forty-six prisoners were forced into the fort's guardroom, an area equaling 18×14.10 feet (or one British square rod), where they were held overnight. In the morning only twenty-three remained alive. Usual explanations for the one hundred twenty-three deaths point to the intense heat and suffocation. But what were the effects of crowding?

Christian (1956) has shown that thyroid and adrenal failure produce death in several species of animals when large numbers are herded into a very small space, even with the temperature remaining at moderate levels. Calhoun (1962) demonstrates that laboratory mice become cannibalistic, sterile, and homicidal when large numbers of them are crowded into a small laboratory box. The term "behavioral sink" has been coined to refer to this degree of social disintegration, behavioral anomaly, and death in the face of extreme crowding.

Human beings have rarely been crowded to this degree. When it has happened, as in the instance of the Black Hole of Calcutta, it has not been examined from a territorial point of view. Nevertheless, there is an association between high degrees of human crowding and higher death rates that are precipitated by both disease and violence. That event in 1756 is but one extreme instance. The plagues of Renaissance Europe occurred at times of rapid population increases in urban centers. In Calcutta and Dacca today there is a similar association between extremely high population density and poverty, disease, natural calamity, and death. In Western cities where police reports and government census statistics are more comparable, high mortality rates and high crime rates occur most noticeably in ghetto areas where the populations are unusually dense. Even here, evidence is mounting (Freedman, 1975) that high crime rates cannot be attributed solely to crowding. It is more an association of high density with poverty that apparently is linked to crime and violence.

Under less extreme conditions, the effects of crowding become even more nebulous. And since the point at which each of us may feel crowded is relative, it is difficult to state precisely what crowding is. Some people feel crowded when there are too many people in the room. One acquaintance would get off an airplane if all the other seats were taken. Yet this same friend rode the crowded subways in New York daily during the rush hours.

Other people feel crowded if the room is full of furniture or if the room is too small. Some students in a test situation at an American university felt crowded if the experimental room was disorderly and dirty, even though only the researcher and subject were present in the room (Goodrich, 1974). These same people did not feel crowded in the same room with several other people when the room was cleaned and orderly. Some of them claimed the room was crowded when the temperature and humidity were high. Others experienced a feeling of crowding when strangers were present.

We've been in ghetto apartments scarcely the size of two rooms in an American middle-class suburban house. The apartments themselves form part of a teeming tenement in a high-population neighborhood. We've chatted with these peo-

ple about the size of the household and the dwelling, and
their replies invariably centered on complaints about the
apartment and the neighborhood. The place is rundown. The
utilities don't function. The superintendent does nothing. The
hallways are as dangerous as the streets. Rarely did anyone
volunteer to complain about crowded quarters.

To be sure, as we raised the question of crowding either
implicitly or explicitly, they would begin to talk about the
apartment being too small. It appeared to us that the respond-
ents were doing exactly what they were being cued for: to
respond. They voiced what the researcher wished to hear.
Crowding became a complaint only when the complaint was
solicited. It is rather like the two mice conversing in the psychologist's lab; one indicates to the other that he now has the
psychologist trained. Every time he presses the lever, the psychologist gives him food. People are congenial. They want to
help. And no matter how expert the expert, informants will
respond to prompting, so that the question itself will determine the response.

There are other tactics. Instead of questions about crowding, we asked wives and mothers in the Bronx what they did
when they wanted to be alone. There were some very interesting replies that told us more about the meaning of the word
"alone" for different ethnic groups.

Women from Italian, British, Jewish, and black American
traditions responded that they would either go out of the
apartment if possible or, as was the usual case, go into a bedroom and close the door. Some complained that because they
had small children it was extremely difficult to find solitude.
What was of interest to us is that they perceived our question
as referring to a desire to gain some measure of separation
from the other family members. It was quite a different matter when we put the same query to Puerto Rican mothers.
They found our question perplexing and difficult to reply to.
Most responded that when they wanted to be alone they went
home to their apartments. They conceived being alone to
mean getting away from strangers and public places. Home
was family and solitude. And solitude meant being close to
their children.

But asking people about crowding or setting up special laboratory conditions for testing people's feelings about crowding is complicated and frequently yields results that tell us very little about crowded living conditions. Our approach relied more heavily on observing how people lived by visiting their homes, placing television cameras in the homes for long periods of time, and studying the flow of pedestrian behavior and behavior in public places. By observing daily activities, we learned just how relative crowding is.

People engage in some activity for a particular period of time. As the number of participants increases, that activity changes or is disrupted: at some point in the increasing density the activity does not continue according to the usual format; at another point it may be discontinued altogether. The participants may begin to complain, quarrel, act independently of the others, or leave. But since the number of possible alternative actions is incredible, it is impossible to define the optimal number of participants for a given unit of space.

People make do if need be. They use their extremities or employ other props to substitute for the usual degree of interpersonal distancing. They invent alternate ways of completing a task or conversation. In some situations they may be jammed to the point of physical discomfort and then ease the tension by making jokes of the matter.

The use of any small crowded space depends not only on the space itself but on adjoining spaces as well. A very small living room can accommodate a large gathering of relatives if each member occasionally moves into the kitchen or bathroom for brief periods. Four children can sleep in a 10-by-12 foot bedroom if they can play, horse around, and do homework in the living room. Rush-hour traffic can be handled by a system of expressways if key local and side streets are not closed for repairs or blocked by some other obstruction.

Crowding in a small space is also relative to other contextual factors such as sex, status, and situation. Some peoples can make do for the moment with smaller spaces. People from another ethnic group would find the same space intolerable for any length of time. Three women can converse

animatedly on a sofa when just the three are present. Put a
man in the middle replacing one of them and the behaviors of
the other two will be drastically altered. Students in a class
can be packed into a seminar room, but the instructor may
become inarticulate if he does not have a space at his back
and to either side. In short, once we leave the murky waters
of how people feel about crowding, we begin to appreciate
the complexity of concepts of crowding and density (see Appendix B).

Tom's family gathering on the beach at Marblehead occurred early in the season. In the early morning hours few
other people ventured out. Shortly after the sun had risen, the
privacy of the beach yielded a feeling of vastness. The pleasure of crossing the street without dodging automobiles was
alone an experience to relax the city dweller. By August the
picture would have been quite different, for Marblehead
would be packed with vacationers, the streets clogged with
automobiles, and the residents grumpy about the hordes of
tourists. Local merchants, however, would anticipate the
influx of tourists and their temperaments might well be
grumpy if the expected crowds did not appear.

At this time of year Tom's family enjoyed the relative privacy the beach afforded them that Sunday morning. Other
gatherings were spaced at comfortable distances down the
beach. But as the morning wore on and the sun warmed the
day, other groups of people also ventured to the beach. By
early afternoon the character of the beach front had altered
significantly as local residents and early vacationers arrived.
The integrity of the family's space was becoming harder and
harder to defend as couples or individuals wove their way
through the various parties on the sand in order to reach the
waterside.

Tom's family had broken into several smaller clusters, as
larger gatherings are prone to do, and every once in a while
someone walked through the space occupied by the larger
family group. Several small children played nearby and their
loud shoutings began to have an obvious effect on the
members of Tom's group. Some glared at the children; others

grumbled about parents who let their kids run wild. On several occasions Tom interrupted his conversation as he turned to look at some sudden noise from the children. At one point, one of the boys ran into the gathering, kicking sand into Tom's group. Tom jumped up and in an irritated voice scolded the boy for not being more careful. Gradually, however, the family's frustration grew more obvious and members began gathering their belongings, and, as they had arrived, left in smaller groupings.

If Tom's family had had an alternative resource, such as swimming, it might have been likely the family would have tolerated the much higher levels of density and noise. As it was, they had gathered for conversation and lunch and the water was still too cold for swimming. The increasing numbers of people appearing on the beach impinged on the previous tranquillity of the family occasion.

Changes in density similarly affect behavioral patterns on public conveyances. Regular riders of the New York City subway system have developed many habits, some of which provide them with privacy and also help pass the time. They've learned, for instance, how to fold a newspaper so that they may read and turn pages but not disturb people sitting on either side of them. During the nonrush hours these passengers may studiously read, ignoring all else. Yet at their own stop they stand and move out of the train at the exact moment it stops, as if wired by some electrical device. This is even more striking if the person happens to be sleeping. Any frequent subway rider can tell the story of someone sitting in the car dozing for twenty or thirty minutes while the subway train moves along, stopping at station after station. At the moment the train halts at his station, the person wakes and without glancing about to verify the stop moves out of the train, fully confident this is his station—which it is.

As rush hour begins and the straphangers crowd in, pressing people against people, these behaviors are modified. People stand jammed against those who are sitting, reducing the exit space to zero. It becomes more difficult to read, and dozing is less frequent, often limited to those who ride to the end stations. One explanation for the change, of course, is that as a result of the crowding the passenger must prepare for his stop by timing his movement through the crowded car to reach an exit safely by the time the train halts.

It is one thing to endure a jammed subway train in which faces will be no more than three inches away and bodies in almost total contact for a duration of twenty to thirty minutes. It is quite another to tolerate such high densities for an extended period of time. During World War II Scheflen was crammed into a troop transport train headed for a port of embarkation. The trip should have taken no more than two hours. It was characteristic of soldiers to endure the crowded conditions with high noise levels and much joking and horsing around. Unfortunately that particular trip took sixteen hours. For some unexplained bureaucratic reason the train was held up at one siding after another. No food was provided, as it was meant to be a short trip. By the end of the third hour, water supplies had also been exhausted.

Gradually joking ceased and tempers flared. Arguments became more frequent and the normal GI complaining took a more seriously bitter tone. The almost continual tactile contact often became unbearable, and what had been joked about a few hours previously occasionally erupted into a fist fight. Some soldiers were resourceful, coaxing several young boys watching the spectacle of a stranded troop train into bringing food and drinks. Others withdrew into themselves and one fellow went berserk, attempting to jump from the train while it was moving. Obviously some adapted to the prolonged crowding and others did not. We are not always sure why, but in this case Scheflen did note that some of the boys who took the conditions poorly were from rural areas. We do know, however, that any statement about crowding must include a reference to duration.

Leaving videotape cameras in households for extended periods provided us with an opportunity to observe without interruption how people use space in the home. Our sample was small by any conventional scientific standards, but the duration or intensity of our observations provided us with an in-depth appreciation of space use.

The apartments occupied by Puerto Ricans were no smaller

than any others in the ghetto neighborhoods we studied. Yet, by black American and British-American standards, Puerto Rican use of the small confined space made rooms seem even more crowded.

Puerto Rican family members frequently congregate in the same room even if pursuing separate activities. Women and small children are often house-bound for much of the day and throughout the evening hours. In fact, in one home the housewife did not leave the apartment during eight weeks of continuous observation. She did permit her two young boys to play in the afternoons under close supervision at the church playground.

Older teen-age boys and adult males in Puerto Rican households leave the apartment for short periods on evenings of good weather. But other family members remain at home. It is not unusual, then, to witness a Puerto Rican family of six or seven huddled closely together in one room for the duration of the evening hours. In one household we recall a regular family event of the children and parents packed onto a sectional sofa watching television. After the children went to bed, the husband and wife would remain on the sofa sitting as close together as before, with their arms about each other.

This habit of sitting close together appears to us to be a rather consistent part of Puerto Rican home behavior. There was, for instance, the case of three young boys sitting together in a single rocking chair watching television. It seemed to make no difference to them that there were other possible seating locations in the room, such as the sofa and floor area. To be sure, their narrow bottoms permitted two to sit on the chair, with the third and youngest sitting on their laps. We watched them thus occupied for most of the afternoon. During a commercial or change in program one or more would get up, stretch, walk about, horse around, or leave the room. But within moments they were back into the rocking chair. Occasionally the youngest would be pushed off the lap of one of his brothers, but after some scurrying around was soon back up, forming the familiar threesome on the rocker.

In apartments of the same size occupied by black Americans, a totally different use of space occurs. Children spread

out over the entire apartment. They regularly move from
room to room, thereby utilizing much of the total space of
the apartment. In the evening hours members of the family
will behave in a similar manner. We rarely observed family
members crowding onto a sofa. If two people sat on a sofa,
they tended to occupy locations at either end. Even when
third and fourth parties entered the room, it would not be unusual for the middle seat to be left vacant. The newer arrivals
would sit elsewhere or leave the room. Black Americans are
large space users. They avoid crowding and disperse in as
much space as is available. British-Americans use space in
very similar patterns, for they also disperse through the available space.

Those of us accustomed to using most of our living space in
the course of an evening become aware of how much we
move about only when we observe for hours the contrast of
Puerto Ricans. We were focusing on space use and thus noticed that black Americans spread throughout the apartment.
But in watching Puerto Ricans in their homes, the differences
seemed even more significant. Black Americans and British-
Americans would undoubtedly experience a great deal of discomfort if forced to interact for long periods of time in the
same space used regularly by Puerto Rican families. The
cramped and crowded territory of the ghetto apartment becomes a conceptually different kind of space as we cross ethnic boundaries.

One activity crossed ethnic lines and appeared in all the
households with children that we studied. Sometimes children
played games of one type or another that carried them into
nearly all rooms of the household. They would chase each
other through the hallways, around cocktail tables, sofas, and
chairs, back into the hallway, through the kitchen, and into
bedrooms. They were large space users at these moments! In
the daytime hours these games would occur with relatively no
inhibition and parents rarely interfered. But this changed in
the evening when all family members were home, and running about was significantly curtailed. In ghetto apartments,
legs of adults and teen-agers sitting in chairs and sofas
blocked nearly all pathways. The noise level also seemed to

be higher and running about would inevitably be called to a halt by the parents. In this instance, one activity crowded that of another.

When is a space crowded? We discovered an elderly Italian man living alone in a three-bedroom apartment. There was very little furniture in the apartment. By no means was he overcrowded. At the other extreme, we found a Yugoslavian family of two parents and five teen-age boys living in a one-bedroom apartment. The living room had been converted into a dormitory for the boys. It contained one bunk-bed set and three single beds. The only other fixture that could fit in the room was the TV set. These people were crowded.

In one black American household, four children, a teen-age girl, and two parents lived in a two-bedroom apartment. There was no dining room and the kitchen was so small that it could fit only appliances and a small table equipped with two chairs. The family had to eat in shifts. This was a crowded apartment. The conventions of family use made it more overcrowded than it was: the children were forbidden to play in the living room during the daytime. Since the bedroom was crammed with beds, they had to play in the narrow hallway. And of course the family had to eat in shifts or carry the food about with them as they ate.

One of the authors lives with his wife and child also in a two-bedroom middle-class Manhattan apartment. Furniture is at a minimum and, except for a corner work area, the one child, despite the repeated objections of his parents, uses the entire apartment, including the master bedroom, as if the whole space is his own turf. He certainly is not overcrowded.

In contrast to urban living, the family in the affluent middle-class suburban home has the use of a living room, dining room, and frequently an eat-in kitchen. This nuclear portion of the residence is supplemented by additional interacting rooms such as dens or libraries, recreational or family rooms, and a sewing or sitting room. There are pantries, utility and laundry rooms, and occasionally in the more affluent homes servant's quarters. There is one bedroom for the parents, and each child will have his or her own bedroom, or if this is not possible brothers will share one room and sisters another. The region will also include an attic and a basement for storage and work areas. There will also be a yard, or what we have called the "surround" of the house.

The yards in our sample averaged 24 square rods, or 726 square yards of open space—this does not include the space occupied by the house and garage. The nucleus (living and dining rooms) had a mean size of 2.3 square rods, or 70 square yards. And the region (kitchen, bedrooms, basement, and other storage areas) had a mean size of 9.4 square rods, or 284 square yards. Total average of the house and lot size (the base) included an area equal to 36 square rods, or 1090 square yards.

Lying at the other extreme is the ghetto apartment. The ghetto residence in our sample averaged only 2.5 square rods, or 76 square yards of total living space. The suburbanite, then, has a living area approximately fifteen times greater than the resident of a ghetto apartment. Contrasting extremes in this instance is not exactly like comparing apples and or-anges. The extremes provide us with a measure of what we are talking about when we discuss overcrowding. Nassau, Westchester, and Bergen counties (which surround New York City) had in 1970 a combined population of about 3,220,000 living in a space of 958 square miles. Manhattan and Bronx counties alone have populations of over 3,000,000 living in a space of 64 square miles.

We could continue this process of comparison for neigh-borhoods, collecting census tract numbers and then dividing this figure into the total area of the neighborhood in square rods, acres, or miles. But aside from their political impact, as we deliberately just instanced above, the results are uninform-ative. Even in the suburbs, where there are relatively uni-form house sizes and yards, it is difficult to make any mean-ingful sense of number of residents per square mile or square block. In urban ghettos it becomes ludicrous. Whole blocks have been torn down for urban renewal; vacant lots are scat-tered throughout a neighborhood; buildings, both commercial and residential, have been abandoned by the dozens, and large warehouses, industrial sites, or parking lots occupy much of the land space of any section of any neighborhood.

The actual amount of space used for residential purposes may be extraordinarily low and difficult to measure, except by the painstaking method of physically counting all residents of only those spaces actually occupied. And then what would this figure actually mean?

Urban neighborhoods may consist of single-family, wood-framed homes with lot size approximating 25 by 100 feet, as is the case in parts of New York City. Or the neighborhood may consist largely of tenement buildings of four to thirty apartments per tenement unit. Many sections of the Bronx and Brooklyn are mixed with single-family homes, tenements, and new high-rise urban renewal projects. Density could vary by block or even within blocks. We could compare this arrangement with portions of Manhattan, where residents primarily live in high-rise luxury apartments.

Urban high-rise buildings can accommodate densities five to ten times greater than can be accommodated in low-rise buildings. And the latter can in turn accommodate about ten times as many residents as a city block containing only free-standing single family homes. But what has been learned about crowding in the process? These kinds of figures make it appear as if some knowledge is being communicated. In the process of offering density as number of people per square unit of land, crowding at the level of the neighborhood is oversimplified and distorted. It can become an extremely useful tool to be twisted by whatever political persuasion is being challenged or promulgated at the moment.

Much more needs to be known about the effects of high-rises and their concentration or scatter placement with low-rises and single-family dwellings. Much more needs to be known about what kinds of high-rises there are, as well as their placement within blocks and neighborhoods. And finally there is the whole question of resources available to a neighborhood regardless of whether high-rises are present or not.

There is the much broader issue of the human population as a whole. The question of an increasing human population brings up two rather contradictory arguments. The first is that of the doomsday prophets. Supposedly recent human population increases have occurred at a geometric rate, while resources, including vital fuels and food supplies, are dwindling. Mass starvation and wars picture a horrendous and catastrophic end for the human species. Judging from what has happened in the past, however, man is quite capable of tolerating massive numbers of deaths, rearranging his political and bureaucratic machinery, and discovering newer technological means of achieving desired goals. This is not to suggest that environmental protection cries are groundless. They are not! We are referring to the survival of the species, and what may well occur is the survival of a significantly diminished world population. The question we have to ask ourselves is: who will be the survivors?

The second position suggests that population increases are not drastic or long term at all. Fostered by Jonas Salk and others, the argument is made that population changes occur as an S-shaped curve, in that the population rate will go up perceptibly for a while and then level off. Of course we are told we are now riding the peak, that population increases are leveling off and we can expect no further crowding. This point of view may reflect an American kind of optimism or base its conclusions on inadequate data. In fact, studies of the five states reporting their recent population figures provide strong evidence of a rise once again in U.S. population (Sklar & Berkov, 1975). Support for an "automatic" leveling off of the human population principally emanates from population studies of nonhuman animals. Such comparisons are to be distrusted.

Other species of mammals, unlike man, still maintain certain population-regulating mechanisms that man has lost. In most other species the density of a population per unit of territory tends to remain relatively constant. Those animals that do not have sufficient dominance to claim a breeding ground within a viable ecological niche of that species migrate out of the territory. They readily fall prey to predators or they do not obtain mates and therefore do not breed. Humans have only one significant predator—other humans. Perhaps more critically humans can breed in almost any kind of territory, however adverse it may be. And through a variety of technological means, they can even make it into a livable space.

Thus when the population of a human territory increases abruptly, people can migrate, but the population-regulating mechanism characteristic of other mammals simply does not have any perceptible effect.

In human history the two major population-control mechanisms have been plague and starvation on the one hand and war on the other. It is still too early to speculate about the potential impact of modern contraceptive measures. There is some indication that birth-control measures may play a role in regulating population, but to our minds the available evidence does not warrant jumping to the conclusion that contraceptive devices will decrease population growth. Kingsley Davis (1967), for example, argues that in some countries of the world population increase is leveling off even though birth-control measures are notoriously unsuccessful. In contrast, he claims, countries in which birth-control measures are considered successful continue to experience an accelerating increase in population.

Plagues have ceased to be a factor in regulating population levels. Wars, however, continue as one instrument of human destruction and act as some measure of birth control. But as the sole means their impact seems to be lessening; population rates continue to rise. An estimated ninety million people lost their lives in Europe during World War II. Yet this horrendous loss of life hardly dented the increases in population on that continent.

We are then faced with an open-ended question: are we in a runaway population takeoff? If so, is this unique to human experience or has it occurred in the past? Put another way, have we had in the history of humanity so huge a population increase, and, if so, what happened? While some of our contemporary population experts have overlooked historical and archaeological records, other researchers are mounting evidence to suggest strongly that areas like the Mediterranean world at the time of Christ must have been experiencing a population increase of incredible proportions. Gideon Sjoberg (1960), the outstanding authority on the city, claimed only a decade ago that the population of Rome at its zenith did not exceed fifty thousand people. Yet Rome probably had a population comparable to urban centers in the contemporary Western world.

A recently excavated provincial Roman capital in Turkey, for instance, yielded a circus maximus larger than the largest contemporary stadiums. Housing for the working-class poor in Mediterranean cities was comparable in space allocation to the nineteenth-century tenements in New York and probably as densely occupied. In the New World we find similar evidence for much larger populations than was previously imagined. Populations in the Valley of Mexico and Mayan urban areas must have reached several million. People lived in urban centers sprawling down from the highlands of Mexico into the Yucatán Peninsula and Petén region of Guatemala very much like the present megalopolises of the Eastern seaboard of the United States.

The puzzle is what happened to all those people. Two centuries before Augustus, the zenith of the Roman Empire, Romans were able to field an army so vast that they could sustain three hundred thousand casualties in three successive battles and still defeat Hannibal. Yet by A.D. 400 a handful of Visigoths were able to sack Rome. Millions of people must have died in the process and many more must not have been born. Still others must not have engaged in sexual union during those first few years we now refer to as the decline of ancient civilization.

High school textbooks and fundamentalist religions stress the rot and evil in the empire to explain Rome's decline. Whatever truth may lie in these kinds of statements, we ought also to include population and the regulating mechanisms of population increases. To many, this may appear as an impersonal or inhuman explanation. We Americans prefer the more comfortable tract that individuals themselves are responsible. Less comfortable is the proposition that a kind of lemming effect may operate to regulate human population.

It is not that plagues, wars, or overcrowding cause population decreases. Such a conclusion would trap us once again in a simplistic view of human events. In the "field" way of seeing, plagues and wars are recognized as mechanisms intimately interlinked with a host of other conditions that play a role in escalating decreases. Thus, whatever the ill effects of crowding may be, crowding alone certainly cannot explain such disasters as the Black Hole of Calcutta, nor can it explain the decline of the Roman Empire. Taken as an isolated explanatory factor, it can't even account for changes in population rates. Crowding is very likely to be associated with poverty, lack of resources, forced immobility, and other deleterious conditions; yet it may also be the case that as these elements reach some critical point a homeostatic mechanism comes into play. The occurrence of overcrowding may be followed by reduced sexuality, sterility, increased mortality, conservation of resources, greater authoritarian means of political control, and some forms of migration. The pendulum would then swing toward rectification before health is adversely affected. In short, we know so little about the effects, if any, that crowding has on the rise and fall of populations.

We are not even sure what crowding really is. What may be seen as crowding in one context, may in another simply be viewed as the usual clustering behavior of human beings. People who assemble in open spaces usually congregate together rather than scattering over the larger area. They leave sections of railway stations, subway cars, beaches, and other public spaces empty while they cluster in much smaller areas. Passengers waiting for trains in the Long Island Railroad Station in Manhattan overcrowd some areas, leaving others vacant, even during the worst moments of the rush hours. Upward of a hundred people will crowd into spaces that often diminish interpersonal space to a foot or so. Yet were the people to spread more evenly over the available space, interpersonal spaces would increase greatly. Ashcraft once observed a man reading a folded newspaper while waiting for his train. Standing around him at close quarters were twenty other people. Had the man moved about five feet, he would have been at the edge of the crowd with an open space of some fifteen feet and plenty of room to read. His behavior might be explained as due to lighting conditions, drafty sections of the station, or the habit of leaving paths free for transit. But, after all this, it is still hard to avoid the conclusion that people simply tend to crowd together.

One example of clustering occurs on superhighways. Especially during periods of adverse weather conditions, there is a regular tendency for automobiles to cluster together, leaving extensive highway spaces vacant. Although explicitly taught in driver training to avoid tailgating and to maximize the space around one's car, people frequently accelerate rapidly when they reach open stretches, only shortly to join a slow-moving pack ahead. Two or three slow-moving drivers may lead a contingent of automobiles that accumulate behind them. Some drivers experience a great deal of frustration at being prevented from traveling at higher speeds. But the interesting point is that despite all their efforts at achieving greater speeds they apparently spend more time in the pack than out of it. The few frantic drivers who escape a pack rapidly cross unused highway space only to join another cluster and begin the process again.

There are also unused spaces in apartments and houses. Even in crowded ghetto apartments, household members use some spaces and do not regularly use others. An efficiency expert might say the residents did not make efficient use of the available space by crowding bulky furniture into the apartment. But efficiency is not what humans always consider when furnishing an apartment. Similarly, just because Puerto Ricans do not use all the available space in a room by no means suggests that the empty or unused spaces are meaningless. Human space cannot be defined on the basis of where the physical body is placed. Unoccupied space may play an important role in determining the definition of occupied space.

The use of space becomes more complicated when one considers the distribution of the human population. Hundreds upon thousands of people left the sparsely populated rural South and Southwest to join an already crowded urban North, Northeast, and West. Our continent is now tipped by the weight of these peoples living in small confined spaces, while vast areas in Nevada, Idaho, and New Mexico are underpopulated. This is also true for the planet as a whole. What faces India, Japan, and parts of North America and Western Europe is counterposed by the unused, underpopulated regions of Mongolia and the Amazon forest. Those of us in the Western world forget there are places where the scarcity is not material resources but people. Therein lies the problem of imbalance.

Part II
REPERCUSSIONS

Chapter 7
SCARCITY

Many Americans dislike crowds. People from rural areas don't exactly mind visiting a city, but are quite relieved that they live where they do. Some suburbanites haven't ventured into Manhattan in over fifteen years, even though they live less than an hour's drive from the city. Some suburban children see the city only if their school plans an excursion trip.

The commuter of course packs himself into the auto or train and makes the daily hour or so journey to and from his job in the city. He may work, eat, and otherwise spend many of his working hours in the city, but he drags his tired bones home to suburbia and his single-family house for the evenings, holidays, and weekends. In suburbia he supposedly leaves behind the crowds, the helter-skelter of corporate life, the rush and push of making a living in a city with millions of other people. There he has a place to park his car without having it ticketed, smashed, or stolen. His wife and kids have a home, a school, a neighborhood free of crime, crowds, and other pressures of urban living. At least so the suburbanite believes. After all, he has soaked anywhere from forty to sixty thousand dollars into a house that also costs two thousand dollars a year in real estate taxes to preserve the illusion that suburban life is better than its urban counterpart.

We really haven't given up our agrarian value that to be close to the land is next to godliness. Cities seem artificial, inhuman. They are damned as havens of all that is evil in mankind. Many think of city dwellers as cold, curt, and impersonal. Although there are no reliable statistical studies to support a notion that violence, poverty, and other social ills are the result of high density, many people continue to believe this is so. But some of the most trouble-free areas of the world have extraordinarily high population densities, the Netherlands, for example. And burglary rates apparently are now higher in the affluent suburban sections of Nassau and western Suffolk counties on Long Island than they are in the much more densely populated affluent Upper East Side of Manhattan.

By itself density is not necessarily the problem it is made out to be. When it occurs with drastically curtailed resources, however, living conditions become intolerable (Freedman, 1975).

Each of us has experienced that unpleasant feeling of being in a crowd when basic necessities are insufficient. Picture for a moment the air-conditioning system breaking down in a crowded theater. As the supply of oxygen decreases and more and more people feel uncomfortable, the performers on stage are unable to hold the audience's attention. If the lavatories, powder rooms, and other areas are also shut down, the atmosphere will be even more offensive. The last straw is when the actors refuse to continue. The audience, cut off from all resources, might well turn into an angry, ugly mob. The key is scarcity of resources.

But this is a problem of temporary scarcity, for the audience can always leave. Much more serious are those situations with chronic shortages of resources. Sometimes these shortages become so acute that large numbers of people die from plague and famine. This problem is faced repeatedly in India, Bangladesh, Ethiopia, and elsewhere. Frequently extensive violence, massive migration, and war accompany this sort of prolonged deprivation, for people are unlikely to remain in their territories while they are in danger of perishing.

One of the most pervasive forms of scarcity in human history is poverty. Poverty is scarcity of a pernicious kind, for it will continue for centuries and will even worsen in the face of rising affluence. During the seventeenth and eighteenth centuries in Britain, for instance, bourgeois indulgences included such new high-priced commodities as tobacco, tea, coffee, and sugar to sweeten beverages. The fortunes of those involved in the trade of these products grew enormously, since the expanding European middle-class population couldn't get enough of these luxury items. England became a prosperous and powerful nation. Yet, in the heyday of this prosperity, Charles Dickens and others decried the obvious social, political, and economic abuses inflicted on a large segment of the population. Britain had long used indentured servitude, impressment into the navy, and transportation to the colonies to help rid itself of massive and worsening urban poverty.

Modern examples of expanding poverty and rising affluence can be found in just about every country of the world. In Mexico, which is well on the road to economic development, the urban middle-class population becomes larger every year. So does the urban poor. Probably the most affluent city in Latin America is Mexico City, with a substantial middle class and one of the worst slums in the world. The United States does not escape this pattern either. There are over twenty million chronically malnourished Americans in this country and, according to press reports of Senate hearings, the number is rising. Each year that the government revises its poverty-level statistics the percentage of people below the poverty line increases, and this occurs even with appropriate statistical adjustments for reporting periods!

Poverty is an explosive issue that all too frequently has been used for political profit. Some blame the conditions of poverty on the poor themselves: people are poor because they are lazy; or they are born that way, it is in their genes; or they are not psychologically equipped to become productive members of society; or they lack motivation. Demagogues have long made political hay with this type of outcry. There are of course the academics, such as Oscar Lewis and Daniel Patrick Moynihan, who make intellectual hay by pursuing some notion that poverty is self-perpetuating. Oscar Lewis, for instance, in promulgating his idea of a culture of poverty, suggested that people growing up in a tradition of poverty know nothing else, that it is ubiquitous and overcomes any potential alternatives. Escape is impossible for all but a handful, and thus people have nothing more to do than pass the same conditions on to their children.

But, like the problems of underdeveloped countries, poverty does not exist nor does it continue in a vacuum. It is not isolated nor independent from the nature of affluence and economic growth. Modern poverty is directly linked with and a response to modern affluence because there is an interdependent relationship between scarcity and abundance.

Just as the Apollo program once mirrored the pride of American technology, so do Harlem, the South Bronx, the South Side of Chicago, Watts, Roxbury, and Appalachia reflect the character of American priorities. It is not that America moved on, leaving these people behind; it is that these people were left behind so that America could move on. They are the satellites that become nodes in a network that had enough funds for a space program, a prolonged war in Vietnam, the construction of superhighways, the construction of Albany malls, Houston Astrodomes, Rockefeller Centers, Bay Area Rapid Transit, and Sunset Boulevards.

Everyone is now cognizant of the meaning of scarcity, that there is not an unlimited abundance for all. Yet what many still do not recognize is that total abundance was never the case. The Horatio Alger stories at the turn of this century or the occasional well-publicized tales of rags to riches were convenient fictions maintaining a myth that America was a land with plenty to be had by all who worked. Too many Americans have long believed that the poor bring the conditions on themselves. But when the idea of scarcity is balanced against the fantastic economic growth of this country, poverty takes on a new meaning. Americans look outside their borders and pity the starving unfortunate millions in other parts of the world. Rarely do they examine the extent to which poverty at home is part of the American way of life. The United States does, after all, have the highest percentage of poor of all the industrialized nations.

When America closed its doors to foreign immigration at the end of World War I, it set in motion a massive migration of millions of people out of the depressed South into the North and Northeast and out of the Southwest into the Pacific coastal states. The new immigration policies meant that for the first time a growing American industry would have to look within its own borders for labor. The industrial sections of this country had always been a magnet for the economically depressed, but the period of the 1920s through the 1950s witnessed significant population shifts in this country, as cities and industry attracted the rural population. The influenza epidemic, prolonged drought, and extreme rural poverty also acted to push Americans out of their traditional rural habitats. *Tobacco Road, God's Little Acre, Native Son,* and a host of other novels pictured this era as no social scientist has. But all the people traded was rural poverty for urban poverty. Coupled with a rapidly rising cost of living, the status of the urban poor has regressed over the years.

This was also a time of expanding wealth. The middle class began to invest in stocks and bonds, purchase vacation homes, and travel to Europe in large numbers. The automobile became part of their way of life. The Depression and Second World War slowed but did not stop progress. It did add casualties to the ranks of the poor and, through the institution of welfare programs, it did lock many people out of the job market and into a state of government dependency. But World War II provided the impetus to industry and technology that was needed to create a widespread affluent society. Leading the pattern of growth were housing and automobiles, but just about every sector of the economy experienced growth.

By the early 1960s, society could afford to send eight million youths to college. The Scarsdales, Walnut Creeks, and Riversides came into their own as suburban living, zoned primarily for single-family dwellings, and began to outstrip urbanites by sheer numbers of people. In 1936 San Fernando Valley was principally populated by grapefruit trees, migrant workers, race-horse ranches, movie studios, and a few wealthy estates. By 1963, it was part of the long suburban sprawl that characterizes the metropolitan growth of Los Angeles.

This affluence was bought by those who had work and managed to keep a steady job. It was paid for by the chronically unemployed and underemployed. At no time during the growth period were there jobs for all who sought work. More critical perhaps were the large numbers of people who did not have steady employment or career jobs with growth built into their annual salaries. In 1962, for instance, one hundred sixty-two applicants competed for one teaching position in a San Francisco suburb. Now in the mid-1970s such examples seem commonplace for today's college graduates. But such examples were always commonplace when the urban poor sought meaningful employment.[1]

During the 1950s, when all this affluence was building, the University of California, a nontuition state-supported educational institution with a yearly enrollment of perhaps a hundred thousand students, accepted high school graduates who earned at least a B average. In addition, applicants had to pass an examination in basic English. High schools in middle-class areas emphasized programs that would enable their students to attend college. In the poorer regions, both in rural Salinas and San Joaquin valleys and in urban neighborhoods, high school programs emphasized general education and work-study so that students could attend high school only on a part-time basis. In an advancing technological society, then, some members of society were being trained to take jobs that required the new types of skills common to professional and white-collar careers. Other members of society were being maintained in an industrially unskilled or semi-skilled environment, one that was rapidly disappearing. Sociologists estimate that 1956 marked the transition from an industrial society of blue-collar workers to a technocratic society of white-collar workers (Bell, 1967). The poor who were being "trained" were being educated for jobs that were obsolete or that provided an income which could not keep pace with the rising cost of living. Once the California Department of Employment retrained some fifty unemployed factory workers in San Francisco as shoe cobblers.

Elliot Liebow (1967) has vividly described the types of jobs that are available, when they are available, for the urban poor. The large percentage are temporary and confined to unskilled heavy construction work. Even when the health of men permitted them to accept this employment, the level of income could not be considered as keeping pace with the economy. Somewhere that growth made a few Americans very wealthy, many more comfortably affluent, and many others very poor. Those employed in growth industries found their incomes surpassing, keeping pace, or just behind rising costs. In any event, their standard of living rose. For the poor, incomes were stagnant and in many cases fell far behind rising costs. The gap between the affluent and poor has steadily widened. One of the most notorious examples is the plight of the West Coast migrant farm workers, who lived in abject misery while their fellow Californians had incomes permitting them to purchase ever more expensive farm produce.

This is the story of scarcity. The process of widening slums, the building of huge ghettos, *bracero* camps and Appalachia, however, is also the story of Scarsdale, Topanga Canyon, Mill Valley, and Newton. It is a story of expanded affluent mobility provided by the car and broadened air travel service. It is a story of increased immobility of the urban poor accompanied by a gradually crumbling and obsolete public transportation system and enclosed and defended suburban residential borders.

Ghetto areas evolve for a variety of reasons. A prevalent myth is that an urban neighborhood begins to deteriorate only when minority and poor citizens move into the neighborhood. But the minority-group poor, black Americans and Puerto Ricans, begin to move into a neighborhood *only* when the rents in that neighborhood begin to fall. How else could they afford to live there? And as rents fall, landlords are increasingly unwilling and unable to provide proper maintenance for their residential buildings. As the processes are set in motion defining a neighborhood as deteriorating, banks and insurance companies are less and less willing to provide home improvement loans or to write policies in the area, and local governments either wittingly or unwittingly begin to decrease services such as street maintenance, trash collection, etc. Within a short time, the neighborhood has effectively become a slum.

When a neighborhood becomes openly recognized as a deteriorated zone, surrounding neighborhoods attempt to close their borders. Openly defensive actions are taken. Typical behaviors of glaring and other monitoring devices discourage crossing borders, and the slum dweller takes physical risks when he crosses into neighborhoods that have set up a territorial defense. Obviously the reverse also holds, and people rightly fear crossing into slum areas. This action serves the dual purpose of preventing migration while at the same time inhibiting the flow of goods and services across the borders of impoverished areas.

Residential mobility does continue, however, and this usually occurs within the various interlinked ghetto areas of an urban center. Thus, for instance, poorer blacks and Puerto Ricans can move out of the extreme poverty-stricken neighborhoods of Manhattan into the slum areas of the South Bronx and gradually make their way into the rapidly decaying sections of Tremont in the East Bronx. Density increases as the numbers of poor people who are trying to escape from the more desperate zones of poverty in the city move to poorer neighborhoods that appear less bleak. Unfortunately the crowding of lower-income peoples into lower-income regions such as Tremont only serves to make living conditions in Tremont worse.

The problem of high density and scarce resources in the ghettos gradually escalates until conditions worsen of their own accord: the higher the density the fewer the resources available to the residents. The fewer the resources the more a ghetto deteriorates and is cut off. The more a ghetto is cut off the more living conditions grow worse. As this occurs, resources will be further reduced. Faced with a poor clientele, merchants begin to shift their interests elsewhere. The reduction of resources embitters residents. Local merchants feel more threatened and alien to the neighborhood. And as crime rates increase, the merchants close down and leave. Health service personnel, maintenance personnel for streets, telephones, and the like shun the neighborhood. Vendors who supply goods and services avoid entering the ghetto if at all possible. Apartments deteriorate as landlords are unwilling to hire maintenance personnel or expend sums to repair fixtures, heating, and the like. This is the tragic story of the South Bronx.

Goods and services that are maintained in the ghetto are not reduced in price. Food is as high—if not higher—in cost as in other areas of the city. The quality of food is also low: bread products taken off store shelves in other neighborhoods and brought into ghetto markets are not reduced in price or marked as day-old bread. As rent collections decrease, landlords put less and less into their properties. One mark of the South Bronx ghetto neighborhood is the overwhelming lack of basic and necessary services. Fuel oil is no longer purchased for the heating system in many apartment buildings. Broken windows are no longer replaced. Radiators are shut off and residents often intimidated into moving out. The rate at which apartment houses are abandoned in New York City is phenomenal. But this is not limited to New York. The Fillmore district of San Francisco may seem more livable only because the weather is milder, but the services inside apartments are identical to those in New York. In St. Louis a new housing project, Pruitt-Igoe, was destroyed by authorities because people would no longer live in it due to the effects of continued vandalism, the presence of junkies, and the dangers in the hallways and stairs.

The extent and repair of public transportation in ghetto areas when compared with other more affluent neighborhoods is striking. The suburbanite living on Long Island outside New York City commutes on a relatively comfortable train, heated and air-conditioned, for an average of thirty to sixty minutes to reach midtown Manhattan. A resident of the East Bronx travels almost an hour on a noisy, dirty, and poorly ventilated elevated and subway train to reach midtown Manhattan. By car the trip takes no more than fifteen minutes in nonrush-hour traffic.

At present only two subway lines service the East Bronx, with a population roughly equal to that of Nassau County on Long Island, which is serviced by a multitude of lines of the

Long Island Rail Road. In addition, it is relatively safe to travel on the Long Island Rail Road as compared to riding public transportation through the ghetto areas of the South Bronx and the Harlem tip of Manhattan. The subway stops are dangerous in the evening, and a resident returning from work walks several blocks to his home through poorly lit streets in high-crime zones. Consequently, more than just a few men are reluctant to travel long distances to work. This hesitation is reinforced by the fear of leaving family members alone in an unsafe apartment building for long periods of time.

A similar scarcity of resources exists within ghetto apartment house complexes. In federally financed housing, project plans must call for the setting aside of walkways and some small zones that might otherwise serve as play yards. But the laws governing the regulation of these projects prohibit closing the project's grounds to people of the neighborhood. No claims, then, can be made on these areas and no enforcement can restrict passage or congregation to the tenants of the project. As a result, frustrated tenants give up treating these areas as their property, since they have no formal means to defend the turf (Newman, 1972). At night these spaces are considered extremely dangerous by all concerned. During the daytime hours parents are very reluctant to allow their children even to play on the grounds unless they can be kept under close and strict parental supervision. As this is frequently impossible, younger children do not take much advantage of these open spaces, which have in fact become no-man's-lands.

It is rather spurious to discuss communal spaces in the ghetto neighborhoods, since residents consider the hallways as dangerous as the streets. Consequently, younger children, especially younger Puerto Rican children, rarely would get the opportunity to play at a neighborhood playground, as their parents keep them apartment-bound as much as possible. The only realistic play spaces in an urban ghetto are the rooftops, fire escapes, and street zones directly in front of the tenement. Even these areas, however, are considered highly dangerous.

The beginnings of the modern ghettos of New York City can be traced to the 1930s, 1940s, and 1950s when apartments were progressively subdivided into smaller and smaller units to accommodate an expanding population of urban poor. Builders and landlords did not invest in new housing to any extent, but simply condensed available living space in the old tenements. Consequently, family activities that were traditionally held in four to six rooms had to be conducted in one or two. What was once a kitchen became the corner of a small room. The other portion of the room served as a living room. It was not the unusual apartment in which the American tradition of a family sit-down dinner had to be abandoned for lack of space. Other traditionally family communal activities had to be curtailed as well, for scarcity forces various activities to vie for available space.

In ghetto neighborhoods this loss of space is compounded by a similar decline in the opportunities for social affiliation. Relatives and visitors simply do not brave the hazards of traveling in and through slum zones, let alone enter a tenement building that is thought to be more dangerous than the streets. Similarly some residents venture out less and less frequently. Family ties often become difficult to maintain.

Thus another kind of scarcity results—the scarcity of affiliates. The scarcity of spouses, lovers, family members, friends, even the scarcity of one's own kind, gives us that unpleasant feeling of loneliness. This kind of scarcity can affect the affluent as well as the poor. We can experience loneliness when in a dense crowd. The mentally ill may experience loneliness when cared for in a large hospital institution.

When the scarcity of affiliates is added to the scarcity of resources, the actual state of deprivation and the feeling of deprivation can feed back on each other, escalating the individual's perception of imaginary and real dangers. Strangers may appear as enemies and customary interactions may be interpreted as threats. Unfortunately in densely populated urban neighborhoods marked by poverty and high crime rates the person who is cut off from friends and relatives becomes, in fact, a sitting target for crime. In lacking associates, the individual is exposed and must depend on his own defenses. Consequently, imagined dangers become real dangers.

Many have experienced that uncomfortable feeling when walking at night down a semi-deserted street in a strange

neighborhood. Hoping to see a policeman or someone trust-
worthy, we hasten our steps, imagining that the transient
shadows of the night harbor those who would do us harm.
We would experience similar feelings if we were alone in
Golden Gate Park at night, or in a parking lot, or the single
passenger on a subway car. The scarcity of people is frightening.

It is not just that the dark alleyway or deserted park hide
the would-be mugger and rapist. The stairs and elevators of
apartment buildings also act as hiding places. Newman
(1972) points out that these locations are the most common
zones for crime in the entire apartment house complex. Stairs,
hallways, and elevators are empty for long hours of the evening. More importantly, perhaps, they are not open to convenient surveillance. No one can see into an elevator or into
or around stairwells. In larger apartment buildings, such as
the modern urban high-rise, Newman argues that the network
of stairways, double-loaded hallways, and elevators yield disastrous results. Unlike streets, these interior networks are
sparsely populated even during the daytime hours, and unlike
the relatively open spaces of the streets and sidewalks, surveillance is next to impossible. The affluent combat this very real
danger with double-entry doors, doormen, elevator operators,
electronic surveillance equipment, and the like. But in mid-
dle- and lower-income housing projects the residents do not
enjoy such luxuries and have often resorted to such drastic
measures as voluntary tenant patrols for the late evening
hours.

Being alone in a building can have a debilitating effect on
our psychological state. Working alone in the evening in a
huge office building may give us a strange sense of echo and
combined with other sounds can make the place quite eerie.
Scheflen recalls once living in an apartment building that was
being converted to commercial use. For several months he
was the only resident in the place. He does not remember any
conscious fear of being alone, but he noticed that he developed the habit of keeping the telephone within reach at all
times.

In ghetto areas it is a fairly common situation for only one or two families to be living in a dilapidated tenement building. The bleakness of the place is overwhelming and the residents live in mortal fear of being attacked. Often the abandoned and unoccupied apartments become havens for poorer squatters, junkies, or youth gang headquarters. Whole sections of some neighborhoods also have been abandoned. Finally, of course, there may be few residents in parts of a ghetto neighborhood because buildings and entire blocks have been converted to warehouses and other commercial and industrial uses. Residents of such blocks then find themselves alone and isolated after the sun goes down.

But even in densely populated regions one can experience a great deal of loneliness and fear if the other people present are different. This is scarcity of one's own kind. Two American tourists may feel terribly uncomfortable walking through the crowded back streets of cities in Pakistan. There are white people who lock their doors and roll up all windows when they must drive through the streets of the Fillmore district in San Francisco, even if it is during daylight hours. Many Puerto Ricans fear riding the subway through black ghetto areas. How many black Americans still believe they take their life in their hands when they walk through white working-class and affluent neighborhoods with no apparent purpose for being there?

Black Americans have some historical reason for fearing potential reprisals if they move through white neighborhoods without having any direct business for being there. White ethnic Americans also have reason to fear in passing through a black ethnic slum area. It is not that the black American will be clubbed down by a red-necked policeman or that the white American will be mugged and otherwise personally violated by a gang of young black toughs. These events do occur, but not with such great frequency to justify the widespread and continuing paranoia. Instead, it is a fear of the unknown. We can generally predict the potential behaviors of our own kind even when they are strangers. Others appear less predictable, especially when they differ in skin color and life style. We are not sure whether they will respect the rights of private property. We are not sure whether they will observe the rules prohibiting public rudeness. We are not sure whether they will acknowledge our rights of privacy and public passage. It is this fearful anticipation of the unknown that characterizes many of our attitudes toward those people who are not one of us.

Some people lose affiliates as they get older. Friends and relatives gradually die; others just seem to drift away for one reason or another. Old age in this country is a time of great loneliness. Some people who are mobile lose affiliates as they move from one place to another. Lack of contact and servicing of the bonds of friendship and family weaken, reduce, and eventually break the old familiar networks. And some of these people are unable to establish new networks or new affiliations once the old ones have been broken. Consequently, older people and persons who for one reason or the other are forced to change jobs or residential locations become potential victims of loneliness, being unable or unwilling to make new friends. They turn inward, often depending totally on their own resources or those of a spouse or immediate family. Others, fearing the loss of attractiveness, earning power, mental acuity, or sexual ability, turn inward upon the loss of a spouse, remaining parent, or sibling. Such insufficiently small and tightly closed networks frequently develop pathological overtones.

The inability to make new contacts is also characteristic of some ethnic groups. In traditional Puerto Rican culture the center of almost all activities and the focus of much of one's network was a large extended family. Women and girls especially grew up in an environment of always being with someone, rarely being alone, never outside the range of some other relative. Aunts, cousins, grandmothers, sisters all would involve themselves in a girl's affairs. Supposedly the good girl, the middle-class girl, never left the household except in the company of another female family member, a chaperone, or in Spanish a *dueña*. This was the ideal.

In reality Puerto Rican girls were often permitted out without a *dueña* if they went in the company of other girls, did not stray far from home, and did not remain away for long periods of time. In the background, however, was that ever-present watchful eye, a nuisance to adolescent girls but never-theless a comfort to the family and a security blanket for the girl. There was a great deal of flexibility in this behavior, even among the middle classes. Yet it appeared as though the large family was all consuming and watchful when compared with families of other ethnic groups. The Puerto Rican "lady" in Puerto Rico was closely bound into a familial network that not only monitored her behavior but also consumed much of her attention. The family was always there as protector, com-forter, and guardian.

The move from the island of Puerto Rico to New York City is far greater culturally and socially than the distance measured in miles. Many Puerto Ricans leaving the island at-tempt to establish themselves in communities where there are numbers of extended kinsmen or at least hometown villagers. Others cannot, and women in particular suffer extreme social deprivation. Even if they do find some extended kinsmen on marriage, they may have to move with their husbands to other sections of the city and thus become cut off from the family. If they can establish a household close to kinsmen, they are better off, but the kinship network will never reach the extent it reaches in Puerto Rico. The pushes and pulls of living in New York City wreak havoc with a thin and frail kinship network.

Puerto Rican women are thus exposed to potentially ex-treme social deprivation. They should not speak with or encourage social intercourse with strangers, especially non-Puerto Ricans. They do not know how to initiate social inter-course, let alone form new affiliations. They are terrified of public transportation, of the streets of the ghetto, and are speechless when confronting the foreign bureaucracy of city agencies. Unwilling or unable to travel to the homes of rela-tives, they find the thin threads of kinship gradually fade in New York. So they stay home, forming tightly cohesive small family units of their own. They are limited almost exclusively to their husbands or immediate family. Sometimes, as is the case in early marriage, their social world is their husband and, should he die or abandon them, they often panic.

To most Americans these women are superstitious, hysterical, and paranoid. If they are referred to the middle-class oriented psychiatric services, they are almost immediately labeled as psychotic or schizophrenic. Many are confined to psychiatric wards. Since Puerto Ricans consider psychoses incurable and dangerous, a patient's friends frequently abandon her. The longer she is confined, the less likely even her immediate family will visit her or take her back. The more her associates drop away, the more she exhibits those behaviors which got her to where she is in the first place.

Although an estimated three quarters of a million Americans are in public hospitals with the diagnosis of schizophrenia, many millions more who are called schizophrenics by psychiatrists live within the general population. Many of these people live alone in high-density urban areas. Some of these people may be unable to replace the original parental object and thus lead an autistic lifelong existence. To picture the heart of their problem as resting solely inside the psyche is to impose on the public an intellectual gibberish that does not serve either the interests of the people or a positively oriented mental health system.

Most diagnostic categories do little more than label people. More credence needs to be given to the relationship between the lack of critical resources such as forced immobility, scarcity of affiliates, inadequate services and crowding, disease, crime, and death. There must be something worth understanding here when so many Americans lead lives drastically different from their fellow countrymen.

Chapter 8
DISINTEGRATION

America is the symbol of change. For better or worse, change affects all aspects of society. Since most of us think change is a good thing, we speak positively of growth, improvement, and development. The New Deal, Fair Deal, New Frontier, and Great Society were master plans for reordering priorities and improving people's lot in life. But change also has deleterious effects. The impact of the period after the Civil War nearly destroyed what was left of the South's economy and did very little for the position of American blacks. Change is not always planned. Certainly the Depression was not a calculated maneuver, nor was our entry into World War I or the Korean War. Yet the upheavals precipitated by these events were tremendous.

Change can be a two-edged sword, for as one group attempts to institute new values and modes of living, another may suffer disintegration. The New York City Planning Commission sought to "change" the closed features of many traditional ethnic neighborhoods by building housing projects or public schools along their borders. The commission hoped to "open" these neighborhoods to other populations, thereby achieving residential redistribution and ethnic integration. But residents thought this policy undermined the neighborhoods' sense of "communty" by precipitating residential instability and ending the old way of life. The style that once gave them distinction would in their opinion decay.

Change coupled with scarcity yields disintegration of a pernicious kind. This is the progressive deterioration of living conditions that occurs as the scarcity of resources available to a population reaches disastrous proportions: forced immobility of densely populated areas, scarcity of jobs and instability of incomes, and scarcity of other resources and affiliations. These are the features of the modern urban ghetto, a neighborhood disintegrated.

Despite all attempts to contain poorer minority peoples within certain sectors of a city, forced immobility has never been totally successful. Witness the spread and growth of the Irish and Italian populations in Boston and the movements of black and Puerto Rican populations in New York City. The thrust outward from areas of extreme poverty proceeds sometimes at a snail's pace and sometimes in great leaps and bounds. Population pressure from within forces some people to move as the increasing numbers of people vie for available space. The pull of those "fringe" zones where decay seems less evident draws the working poor out of the severely deteriorated zones as they seek to pool their meager resources and move to better and safer housing.

A similar process occurs in the border areas of working-class neighborhoods as these people try to retreat from poverty and the "invasion" of peoples of other ethnic backgrounds. Some marry up and out. Some raise their incomes through a college education or a union-controlled trade. Some retire and move nearer their children who have left in search of economic success. In almost all instances, the direction of working-class peoples is to get out of the city and into the suburbs. There are those who say they are running from the evils of the city. There are those who say they want a yard and a real home. Whatever the reasons, large numbers of working-class Americans have been moving into the suburbs since World War II at an ever-increasing rate, depleting the population of the city and leaving sections inhabited almost totally by the poor. This is what has been happening in the Bronx.

The history of the Bronx in New York City is a story of all these changes. Unfortunately, for large sections of the South Bronx, it is a story of change leading to massive urban decay. The details may be peculiar to the population shifts of the Bronx and New York City as a whole, but the patterns of territorial disruption and population changes are representative of many American cities, and, for that matter, some sections of the country as well.

In the Bronx the population declined rather sharply from the close of World War II until around 1960. The decline was most marked by the exodus of massive numbers of younger families and marriageable adults of the traditional white ethnic population. Younger Americans of Jewish, Irish, British, German, and Italian descent have been fleeing from the city. They are being replaced by the northward movement of Puerto Ricans and black Americans who are also attempting to escape from severe poverty and high crime. Only their story is different, for they are limited in movement and in some cases may have reached the end of the road.

Such movements are not new to American history, for as each new wave of immigrants arrived, the older ethnics were in the process of both relocating and moving a rung or two up the social and economic ladder. Some sections of American cities have more directly reflected this migration pattern than others. The Bronx is a part of this larger picture, for it is in the patterns of migration that an appreciation for neighborhood disintegration is gained.

The growth of the Bronx is inextricably linked to the growth and rising fortunes of Manhattan. The opening of the Harlem Bridge and the old Boston Road, which ran through the Bronx in the late eighteenth century, provided an active stimulus for exurban settlement. The railroads in the mid-nineteenth century added icing to the cake, and the Bronx was forever more locked into a residential pattern tying it to the metropolitan center of New York City.

Most of the early settlements during this critical period were made by working-class peoples who found housing along the railroad lines. The first major wave of residents were the Irish and Germans, who moved into the Bronx after the opening of the Harlem Railroad in the mid-nineteenth century. By the time of the 1910 census, Germans and Irish were spread over the entire Bronx County in considerable numbers. It was at about this time that Italian immigrants began to move into the Bronx along the railroad lines, replacing Irish and Germans who moved farther northward. Later, immigrants from Eastern Europe settled in the southern Bronx and the Italians themselves migrated into the central Bronx region. By the 1920 census, peoples of Eastern European descent had replaced the other populations as the dominant ethnic group in the South Bronx, their numbers reaching over twenty per cent in some areas.

By the Depression period, the population of the Bronx had passed the one million mark, with working-class and lower-class immigrants forming a large percentage of the total. The character of the Bronx was thus set early in its history. Successive waves of newer and poorer immigrants moved into the South Bronx, first settling into the tenements along the railroad lines and then gradually spreading outward into the entire South Bronx area. Older ethnics retreated northward in search of better housing and others resisted attempts to integrate their neighborhoods. This northward migration pattern also meant a shift upward economically, even if this was only a minuscule jump.

The center for the Bronx was and is Manhattan. The physical characteristics of the Bronx are still largely the result of nineteenth-century developers who built the region as a working-class suburb to accommodate an expanding Manhattan population. Even today a resident can more easily reach Manhattan by rail or car than he can cross the Bronx. Most of the present structures were built to house the immigrant populations that were spilling over the Harlem River.

For most of the South Bronx, housing was mainly tenements, with the flimsier models being constructed along the railroad lines to house poorer residents. These early tenements already hinted at the fact that the South, Central, and East Bronx neighborhoods were primarily designed as economy measures and not according to other factors. The Bronx as a periphery of Manhattan was certainly not to become the suburb which marks today's communities zoned for single-family housing.

World War II and its aftermath changed the character of the Bronx's population, but in no way altered the pattern of migration flow. The so-called newer ethnic minorities of blacks and Puerto Ricans gradually began crossing the Harlem River in increasing numbers during and after World War II. They first moved into the subdivided and low-grade tenements lying along the elevated lines in the South Bronx. Then, like the ethnic immigrants before them, they spread outward throughout the South Bronx and then gradually northward into the Central Bronx region.

By the 1950s, the majority of older ethnics had moved out of the South Bronx and were beginning to abandon regions of the Central Bronx. The black population, for example, which equaled less than one per cent of the population of the Central Bronx in 1950, rose to 33 per cent by 1970. Puerto Ricans and blacks comprised nearly 40 per cent of the Bronx population by 1966, compared with about 24 per cent in 1960. The New York *Times* analysis of the 1970 census data indicated that the residential impact of the combined black and Puerto Rican increase in population for New York City was felt primarily in the areas peripheral to established minority settlements. That is, despite all attempts at containment, the decade from 1960 to 1970 witnessed extremely sharp population changes in such areas as the Central Bronx.

Tremont is a loosely defined neighborhood in the Central Bronx, where the ethnic shift is thought to be the greatest over the past few years. Our demographic survey revealed that only about 11 per cent of the population was Italian, with some 18 per cent being other white ethnics (mainly Eastern European Jewish, Irish, and German). Forty-seven per cent of the population was Puerto Rican and about 23 per cent was black. Approximately 61 per cent of the sample were native-born Americans, with over 25 per cent born in Puerto Rico.

The population changes also indicated that the Tremont section was becoming younger, with some 28 per cent under twenty years of age. Analysis of our sample material demonstrated very clearly that the black and Puerto Rican migrations were flowing outward from the area immediately adjacent to the Tremont region. The same patterns were then reproducing themselves; only the names of the people were changing.

For the purposes of illustration, Tremont can be divided into two subneighborhoods of East Tremont and Belmont. East Tremont is now characterized by an overwhelming preponderance of blacks and Puerto Ricans. The area is experiencing rapid urban decay on a large scale. Along the northern borders of East Tremont lay the remaining elements of an Italian enclave called Belmont. It is principally peopled by working-class Italians, though recently some Albanians and Yugoslavian immigrants have moved in along the southeastern border.

The New York Central Railroad and the now discontinued Third Avenue elevated train were critical factors, not only contributing to population growth but also to its physical structure as well. Traditionally the villages of Belmont, East Tremont, Treford, and West Farms formed the larger Tremont section. These areas grew up in the last quarter of the nineteenth century. But already by 1900 the boundaries of these older villages were disappearing as a result of development schemes and population inflow which resulted in a carved-up landscape. Housing was quickly and cheaply thrown up to cater to the flow of European immigrants moving out of Manhattan, and the older villages were evidently replaced by the urban neighborhoods of Belmont, East Tremont, and Treford.

Each successive wave of immigrants has steadily worked to disembowel the boundaries of even these neighborhoods. The massive northward push of blacks and Puerto Ricans for all practical purposes marked the end of the traditional community boundaries. It is not that these changes can be attributed to the people themselves, for a series of events fostered by land speculators, politicians, and city planners have systematically worked to break up traditional neighborhoods. Consequently, what the New York City Planning Commission euphemistically calls the Treford neighborhood is nothing more than an extension of the black and Puerto Rican ghetto of East Tremont. We could find no evidence of a remaining sense of a Treford community. Only Belmont holds out as an Italian enclave, even if its borders do continue to shrink.

East Tremont lies to the north of the severely deteriorated neighborhood of the South Bronx. While both neighborhoods are predominantly, if not totally, black and Puerto Rican, East Tremonters do in fact maintain a distinction. They see themselves as less depressed economically and socially. In fact many of them moved north into East Tremont to escape worse slums of the South Bronx. Some of them view East Tremont as an end of the road. Others still hope that they can make the jump out of extreme poverty. This distinction may soon be moot, since East Tremont is well on the road to joining the South Bronx as a deteriorated neighborhood of the worst kind.

For all practical purposes East Tremont's southern border is now delineated by the Cross Bronx Expressway. The traditional boundaries used to extend a few blocks farther south, but the construction of the expressway cleared a swath of land transecting East Tremont proper from its southern border regions. Some of the people on both sides of the elevated highway consider this separated section still part of East Tremont. But the physical barrier is ominous and time seems to consign the smaller section to the South Bronx. This separation, as well as the noise of the traffic, is a source of many complaints. When the highway was built, many social and familial networks were disrupted and a good deal of bitterness developed as a result.

To the west of East Tremont is the Grand Concourse strip, with a population consisting largely of peoples of middle-class and lower middle-class Eastern European Jewish descent. They literally hold the line along the entire western border. The Grand Concourse was once the well-to-do boulevard of a prosperous suburban Bronx. This highway is lined with more expensive apartment houses, which by the nature of their layout strongly hint at an early enclave. Puerto Ricans and blacks have moved into the streets lying adjacent to this strip, but, in contrast to the Grand Concourse iself, they live in poorly preserved and subdivided tenements. They may exist only a half-block away, but they could be worlds apart socially, economically, and in terms of housing.

The Jewish enclave on the Grand Concourse is thus a half-block in width but several miles in length. If one drives up the Grand Concourse, the neighborhood seems prosperous. The buildings are well preserved and the streets are clean. But if the same driver turns off the boulevard, he is instantly in an urban slum within the range of a few houses. The buildings are seriously deteriorated. Garbage and trash collections and street cleaning are not carried out with any regularity. Jewish residents evidently restrict their movements in the neighborhood to the Grand Concourse, for they avoid the back streets with terror.

The eastern border of East Tremont is just as interesting. Here lies the neighborhood of Parkchester, a slightly more prosperous white neighborhood than East Tremont. Residents of Parkchester wage a vigorous defense against any residential incursions by blacks and Puerto Ricans. They are aided in this battle by a no-man's-land, superhighways, and currently projected urban renewal plans that physically separate the two adjoining neighborhoods. Clearly much more is at work than American tradition to define a territory, as the Bronx River, Bronx River Parkway, Cross Bronx Expressway, and the East Tremont Avenue elevated train crisscross the border areas. Added to this are five to six blocks of vacant land, an area supposedly being designated for urban renewal. On other streets, for block after block, auto junkyard meets auto junkyard, which in combination with some commercial warehouses and abandoned commercial buildings remind one of a no-man's-land in a war zone.

The northern borders of East Tremont represent the present battlegrounds, for it is into the traditional Italian neighborhood of Belmont that blacks and Puerto Ricans have made any successful penetration. We have alluded to this problem in previous chapters, but it is worthwhile pursuing the example in detail here.

From the Italian perspective the threat is one of annihilation of a traditional neighborhood, a neighborhood that has been steadily shrinking anyway. There is the frequently heard cry of "enough." From the other perspective, that is, of blacks and Puerto Ricans, movement into Belmont is the only possible alternative to escape the ever-developing slum of East Tremont. To the south lies a worse slum; to the east is a militantly antiblack white neighborhood, which in combination with the empty border blocks exposes the individual black family to the hazards of extreme racism. To the west is the narrow Grand Concourse strip with more expensive housing, where, even if apartments were available, which they are not, very little housing relief would be offered to the Tremont population. The direction is north—that traditional line of march in the Bronx. The direction is Belmont, where only a street or a few public buildings divide the Italian enclave from the black and Puerto Rican enclaves. Thus the confrontation. One side attempts to prevent invasion and the potential disintegration of their neighborhood. The other side tries to move out of a disintegrated neighborhood into what appears to be better housing.

Because the borders between blacks and Puerto Ricans on the one side and Italians on the other have shifted so many times over the past few years, it is difficult to fix the old neighborhood lines. Neighborhoods were more often defined by ethnicity than by geographical borders.

East 180th Street runs east and west and for some years acted as the border between East Tremont and Belmont. But the northward push of families out of East Tremont has now resulted in a crossing of this earlier barrier and an occupation of Belmont's old turf as far north as 184th Street. The newcomers were aided in this border crossing by an urban renewal scheme that deliberately cut across the traditional boundaries. This plan cut into the Belmont border area, tearing down tenements and erecting newer urban high-rise buildings. It took some ten years to complete, as Italians and other white ethnic groups fought a rear-guard action. But it was finally completed. Despite promises to the contrary, only lower-income peoples could move into the buildings, as mandated by federal guidelines. This precluded Italian and middle-income black occupancy. Consequently, Twin Parks is almost exclusively occupied by lower-income blacks and Puerto Ricans.

Many of the black families who have bridged the 180th Street border continue to identify themselves with East Tremont, and to some measure this ethnic identification reflects the racial disagreements between the primarily black and Puerto Rican ethos of East Tremont and the Italian culture of the Belmont region. But this value does portend unfavorable conditions for any prolonged continuation of a Belmont neighborhood. Complicating the issue are the few moderate-income black families who have taken up residence on the fringes of the Italian community. They do not identify themselves with their poorer southern neighbors, but they in turn are not accepted by their Italian neighbors. As the situation deteriorates further, there is little hope that traditional communities will survive. The disintegration of Belmont is well on its way as younger Italians leave. Older residents remain to watch house by house give way to what they openly refer to as enemies. It is likely that Belmont will gradually become submerged into a larger East Tremont neighborhood with a predominantly black and Puerto Rican population occupying many of the blocks of what once was the community of Belmont.

Central and Western Europe experienced similar waves of migration a thousand years before Christ. Celtic peoples moved westward across Europe and on into what is now Ireland. In the face of these massive migrations older ways of life disintegrated and were replaced by or interwoven with a Celtic culture. Celtic peoples also moved to the south into the Italian and Greek peninsulas, conquering and looting as they went. Later waves of other peoples rolled out of Central Europe into the southern regions. And, still later, bands of Visigoths carried their military excursions southward. From the viewpoint of the literate Greeks and Latins, the invaders were monsters, a not unsimilar epitaph laid at the feet of migrating blacks and Puerto Ricans. Yet, seen from the other side, many of these peoples were being pushed either by other invaders or as a result of climatological changes that brought long periods of drought and famine. They were seeking food and relief from extreme poverty, overpopulation, and high-scarcity problems. The migrations across the Harlem River into the South Bronx and then up into East Tremont and Belmont reflect corresponding concerns.

In short, there is a point at which the presence of so many unemployed and poverty-stricken people acts like a pressure release, catapulting individuals and families across even the most heavily defended borders. When this occurs, the traditional organization of the adjacent territory will be disrupted.

Thus far we have pictured migrations as involving the physical movement of people, much like the features of an invading army. There are other kinds of migrations that can upset stability and help precipitate a disintegration of traditional patterns. There are, for instance, the flow of ideas, ideologies, economic style, and the like. The spread of Buddhism into China and later Japan had a tremendous impact on the lives of the people involved. One legacy of Cortez was the introduction of the horse into the New World. The migrations of this animal northward into the Great Plains region of North America drastically disrupted the traditional life style, economy, social organization, and culture of the Plains Indians. Another legacy of the Spanish Conquest of Mexico was the gradual but persistent northward march of Catholic missionaries who settled into one region after the other, building missions, converting and colonizing Indians, and introducing farming as a new means of making a living. Traditional Indian society never recovered. By the time North Americans moved westward in large numbers in the nineteenth century, Indian culture and society were significantly different from what they had been in the days before the horse and the Spanish missionary.

In the modern world political ideologies spread their sphere of influence over vast tracts of territories without physically invading the country. The United States has in one form or the other and at one time or the other dictated the politics and economics of every Latin American country. In recent years the United States has fostered changes of government and preserved certain class structures in Guyana (British

Guiana), Guatemala, the Dominican Republic, and most recently in Chile. Though we had no troops in the old Belgian Congo, we diverted millions of dollars and exercised every means possible, including assassinations, to develop the government we desired.

Corporate empires act along similar lines, influencing not only markets favorable to their ends but also governments and other local interests to create favorable market conditions. At the end of World War II, much of the European economy was either owned by or influenced by American-based firms. The American Fruit Company and the United Fruit Company, now conveniently expanded into a larger holding company known as United Brands, dictated not only the course of governments but also laid the very foundations for people's economic survival. In one banana-growing region after the other, the presence or withdrawal of either one of these companies meant boom or bust for even the most remote peasant. "Banana republic" was a name meaning more than just control of local politicians. It also meant control over the local populations.

Within the United States governmental system there are a number of federal and state agencies that crisscross local government agencies and influence the lives of neighborhood residents. Any city not only has its district attorney, but will also be within a region controlled by the state attorney general and a region controlled by a federal attorney. Supposedly their jurisdictions and duties do not overlap, but in fact they often do. It was a territorial argument that created much of the confusion surrounding John F. Kennedy's assassination. Congress then imposed its will on local governments and resolved the matter in favor of the federal jurisdictional system. Thus the recent attempts on President Gerald Ford's life in 1975, though criminal acts that normally would fall under local jurisdiction, were, in fact, prosecuted by federal attorneys in federal courts.

Federal, state, and local narcotics agencies pursue the same criminals with vigor. The agencies of the Treasury Department, including the Bureau of Internal Revenue, are matched in some states by a state-level income tax agency and investigative unit, and in New York City by a city-level income tax agency and investigative unit. State health agencies carve up the local regions, extending their influence into the health treatment of local residents. On top is a federal health bureaucracy that monitors all health-related activities and to some extent also extends its influence into the immediate lives of the local citizens.

Almost any urban neighborhood in the United States must surrender some of its territory to the maze of state and federal agencies that extend a hand into the living patterns of local neighborhood residents. Some resist the intrusions from the outside. Local congressmen frequently become outraged when some bureaucratic mix-up has upset the lives of some of their constituents. But they get just as upset if, like United Brands, the federal government attempts to pull out of an area or does not pump federal money into the congressman's pet local projects.

Thus migrants, ideologies, representatives of foreign or larger territorial organizations, and even technology act as agents who may disrupt the stability of a homogeneous population. These agents of change undoubtedly run against customs and occasionally laws, and the infractions can lead to antagonisms, hostility, violence, and prosecution within the territory. They disrupt the patterns; they do not necessarily in and of themselves also disrupt the physical features of the territory. Admiral Perry's arrival in Japan threw that country into a revolution which was to have repercussions around the world. But the borders of Japan remained intact.

It is possible, however, for these agents acting in concert to confuse and break down conventional physical boundaries. The clearest example is the establishment of multiple layers of local, state, and federal bureaucracy. When these various agencies finish defining a given piece of turf, one wonders if any integral territory can remain in this country. There are the political wards and precincts that have to do with voting and politics. These rarely conform to the precincts established by local police. Then there is the post office with its postal zones. The health departments establish their health or catchment areas. There are, of course, multiple civil and criminal judicial systems. About the time the concerned citizen masters all the zones in which he lives, an election will bring in a new group of good guys and the whole arrangement will be gerrymandered in a different direction. It is the wise man or the fool who can provide some answer to the question, "Where do you live?" Unfortunately these political divisions rarely conform to the boundaries that evolved to define a neighborhood as a community.

Advancing technology has repeatedly disrupted territories in this country. In the second half of the nineteenth century railroads were built across America, carrying with them rights of way that transected many an established location, from small farms to villages, towns, and cities. The consequent human suffering seemed of less concern than the need to have a transportation system commensurate with the political-economic interests of the day. Twentieth-century America lives with its obsolete railroads, but leaves the rights of way intact and extends a new superhighway network across the land, doing better and more efficiently what its nineteenth-century counterpart did on a Lilliputian scale.

The construction of highways not only forces families to move and set up roots in a new location; it also divides friends and relatives, helps to isolate those who have difficulty forming new associates, and acts to the benefit of those who would maintain ethnic and class boundaries or contain ethnic and class migration. In Philadelphia, for example, the planning of one expressway was based on an obvious attempt to contain blacks living to the south of the proposed route by providing a barrier that would prevent them from entering the more affluent white neighborhoods to the north. When this fact became public knowledge, many citizens rose up in anger and launched a successful campaign that eventually halted plans to construct Philadelphia's version of the Chinese Wall.

In New York it is easily possible for the affluent suburbanites of Westchester County and beyond to pass through the Bronx on their way to New York City by car or commuter train without being exposed directly to the people living in the Bronx. Expressways cut through the Bronx, remaking the character of the old immigrant neighborhoods. Friends and relatives who once lived as neighbors have been separated. People who have no hope of escaping to suburbia must endure the noise and air pollution of their suburban commuting neighbors as they pass overhead along the multimillion-dollar superhighways that have formed a cornerstone of American postwar affluence.

The original territorial designation of divisions, neighborhoods, towns, and counties, which formed a great part of American geopolitics, has been disrupted. The repeated processes of rebordering traditional territories either through political chicanery or land speculation, of transecting territories with major routes, and of restructuring local places to represent the interests of industry, commerce, and government have left us with highly ambiguous and confused networks of urban neighborhoods. It would be a gross misnomer of the worst kind to picture urban residential areas as communities in any traditional meaning of that word. How could we then expect people to protect, defend, monitor, clean up, and hold on to the areas in which they live? They live in a transitory hodgepodge that is like forever living in each of the various nodes of the Holiday Inn motel network. Somebody else prepares and takes care of the room.

When peoples of many institutional memberships, social classes, and ethnic backgrounds live in the same territory, a great deal of ambiguity often prevails about laws, customs, and territorial respect. If a housing project is built in a stable and traditionally ethnic neighborhood, those who have lived there may resent the loss of neighboring houses and their right to use certain streets. They are likely to refuse to acknowledge the territorial integrity of the project. They will freely pass through it; they may allow their children to play on the grounds and turn an unconcerned face away as teenagers congregate on the sidewalks obstructing the passage of project residents and even intruding on their rights of privacy.

There are times when nonlocal governmental agencies occupy sites in a particular neighborhood. The results may erupt into difficulties over jurisdictional disputes. Who is in charge, the local branch manager or the locally based regional man-

ager? Who has jurisdictional control over local citizens working on a nearby military base and what freedom do the military police enjoy to search and seize property or the bodies of
people who are not on the base, but who are employed there?
These questions can pose serious problems for local residents
and authorities. There is, for instance, a large state hospital
located in a particular neighborhood of the Bronx. Since the
hospital's grounds are state property, there is a jurisdictional
problem among the state, city, and local hospital security
guards. Certain complex arrangements have been established
which permit some modicum of sensibility, but not totally.
The hospital security police can issue New York City traffic
tickets by reporting to the local police station. But since neither security police nor New York City police have the right
under state law to make arrests on state property, the State of
New York must pay two state patrolmen to remain on the
hospital grounds.

There are greater degrees of bureaucratic absurdity and
ambiguity that make it difficult to maintain public order. Economic arrangements also become the target of hatred among
the urban poor. There is a continuing low-level kind of hostility in urban slum zones against the absentee owners of housing, businesses, and commercial enterprises. At times of civil
unrest this hostility frequently erupts into a more overt and
active anger. Black Americans who own businesses in the
ghettos become targets as well. Attempts were made by some
in the years of recent riots to distinguish black ownership
from white by putting up signs on the business windows
claiming to be a "soul brother." In the history of the United
States similar events have occurred at a national level. The internment of German nationals living in America during
World War I and the confiscation of property and internment
of individuals of Japanese descent in California at the out-
break of World War II are classic cases in point.

The problems of modern territoriality are reflected in the
heterogeneous mix of any urban scene. Living side by side in
adjacent houses in the same block or in adjacent apartments
in an apartment building may be blacks, Puerto Ricans, and
Italians. Different life styles impinge on and sometimes come

into conflict with one another. The cues and shared codes that are part of the armor of a homogeneous culture are misinterpreted and noninterpreted by peoples of another culture. The housing itself may be owned by someone else of a different ethnic group and social class. The owner's understanding of renters will be based on his own viewpoint, while renters may interpret his behavior as foreign, cold, and commercial. Anyone who lives in a heterogeneous territory is therefore at any one time living under different but simultaneous jurisdictions and traditional patronages which in their ambiguity contribute to disintegration, instability, and occasionally violence.

Chapter 9
VIOLENCE

Violence is hypnotic. As Shakespeare's *Richard III* comments, violence feeds on violence with all the irresistible charm the human intellect can muster. In America and Western Europe there remains a pervasive fascination with the violent, even if the desire to experience its sweet taste is only at a distance. Movies such as *A Clockwork Orange* and *Jaws* pander to the spectator who can thrill at events removed from the present self. We civilized beings look to this violence as if it occurs among others, not ourselves. It belongs to fiction, film, TV. In Vietnam soldiers returning from a battle often responded to interviewers' questions with the comment that the fighting was just like on TV. Blacks are violent. Latins are hot-tempered. A few years ago we thought the most inhumane people on this planet were the Japanese. Propaganda pictured their soldiers as sadistic, brutal rapists of women and murderers of children. Germans ran in a similar mold. Our soldiers were the rescuers.

Occasionally, however, we do permit glances at ourselves, glances at a fantasy of a little homunculus of a creature, wild and animal-like, buried deep inside us. It is a primordial self, conveniently repressed and suppressed, shielded by a strong cloak of civilization. And so in films such as *Deliverance, Joe,* and *Straw Dogs,* we see the mask of civilization stripped, leaving bare the violence thought to be so much a factor in our primitive selves. This violence lies hidden, to be called up in the most extreme moments of defense, a defense occasioned by threats to the self, to our loved ones, or to values that we cherish.

Yet where in nature is the source of this belief in a primordial violent self? What anthropologist has discovered a primitive people more violent than everyday urban man? What ethologist finds violence as a way of life among animals? If not in nature, then it must rest solely in our civilized fantasy of nature.

In the "wilds" of nature it is less the act of violence and more the threat of violence that marks the behaviors we so frequently picture. The ferocious-looking canines of baboons, the beating of the breasts by gorillas, the raised hair on the back of the neck of a dog, the pawing of the turf by a wild mustang are behaviors meant to give pause. In many cases they are simply warnings that a territorial border has been crossed. Recourse to violence is a much rarer act than we in our media-inspired imaginations tend to recognize, since creatures in nature rarely kill their own species. In fact, the threatening displays avoid violence instead of escalating it.

In the conventional wisdom of everyday America, one of the stock explanations for violence implicates the personality, motives, or violent nature of those who participate in the violence. Psychiatric experience indicates that a particular kind of personality may suddenly and unexpectedly explode into violence. This personality type is usually male, one who has long been introspective, introverted, quiet, and previously peaceful. He may have been viewed as odd, strange, distant, or a loner by the people who knew him well. There were no previous indications of violence. Studies of the families of these people often point to an immobilization of the individual precipitated by dominant parents, excessive loyalty, and a high level of dependence. In response to the expectations of a lonely mother, for example, some of these men have been unable to move upward on the social scale. They may have avoided attending college or failed to complete college, or neglected to seek the more financially rewarding employment possibilities. They have no friends or associates. They have avoided relationships, sexual or marital, with the opposite sex. These people have been locked into a very sticky one-to-one relationship with one parent. The act of violence, then, is sometimes directed at this person, or sometimes at others outside the family.

There is another kind of person that psychiatrists suggest is prone to violence. This person has had a history of poor or weak institutional affiliations with family, church, school, clubs, or governments. He is rather self-centered and relatively free from the doctrinal enculturation of these institutions. He is probably labeled aggressive and antisocial, but is usually withdrawn, autistic, or unable to relate closely with others. On probing into his case history, however, it is frequently learned that he did have associations, but that they were with teen-age street gangs and later with criminal teams or organized crime. In his adult life he often lives in the crevices of urban society, enjoying the style of an underworld culture and sallying forth to commit crimes of violence for money and profit or revenge and protection. Since the world of the majority rarely recognizes or respects the territories of this covert world, those who inhabit the back alleyways of society are likely to do violence to anyone who intrudes wittingly or unwittingly on their turf.

There is a third type who is prone to violence. He is the strong advocate of using violence to solve any interpersonal problems. In literature and film this stereotype in America has come to be associated with those Sicilian-Americans involved in the various branches of organized crime: the Mafia, the Cosa Nostra, etc. In other societies, such as ancient Iran and China, there were similar organizations of assassins who worked for one employer or the other. There are also examples of those who are attracted to a long-standing political struggle that employs violence as a means of reaching a desired goal. The Tupemaros, the Mau Mau, the FLN in Algeria, the Viet Minh in Indochina attracted fodder of this type. Included in this type must also be those who are attracted by some sort of religious fervor to employ any means to achieve an end. These are the people with authoritarian personalities and very high F scores on the personality ratio (Adorno, et al, 1950) who become the thugs for the Black Shirts in Germany and whatever other colored shirts in Selma, Alabama, in Chile, in Greece, in Brazil. They are self-righteous and feel perfectly justified in any action they take. They all too often gain an institutional backing, for they are prone to filter themselves into the police, military, or para-military organizations.

Another common explanation for violence is to blame an ethnic group. Violence is thought to be part of their nature or part of their upbringing. It is true that some peoples have a history of aggressive warfare or provisioning someone else's army with mercenaries. The traditional Nuer of the Sudan were long feared by their neighbors as warlike and aggressive. Prior to Pax Britannia, the Nayar of southern India excelled as a caste of professional warriors open for hire. The hordes of Mongols racing into China proper or into Eastern and Central Europe are pictured in history as bloodthirsty savages. The Prussians at one time in history were known as having well-trained mercenaries who would do war for the right price. Yet today we can picture the Nuer, Nayar, Mongol, or Prussian in a totally different light. If a people are warlike in one century and peaceful in another, then aggression can hardly be an instinctual or racial characteristic.

In contemporary America, fear, hatred, and demagoguery are promulgated by those who would picture black Americans as violent, as potentially hazardous to the public order, as people who will rob, steal, and commit homicide if left un-controlled. A century ago the same characterization was given of the Irish who settled in large numbers in the cities of the Eastern seaboard. Roughly one hundred fifty years ago black Americans were described as childlike, lazy creatures who if left alone would do nothing but sleep under a willow tree. If we were to employ the nonsense of the Jensen-type theory builders, then we would guess that some fantastic genetic mu-tations have occurred over the past several generations chang-ing black Americans from passive, carefree, and silly darkies to aggressive, angry, and violent blacks.

But after listing the types of people who are often implicated in acts of violence, we still have not touched on the issue of violence itself. Most people get caught up in violence on only a single occasion in their lifetimes, and almost anyone can become violent under certain conditions. Everyone has his or her breaking point. It is more fruitful to explore the contexts in which violence occurs.

There are those who would picture this context solely in terms of urban high-density living conditions. Yet crime and other forms of violence are not dependent on population density or crowding alone. In fact, crowding or high density rarely exist separately from other critically important factors such as poverty and scarcity (Freedman, 1975). Crime occurs with greater frequency in crowded, poorer neighborhoods and to a lesser extent at the common borders of poorer and more affluent neighborhoods. From this perspective, a common line between the Irish of a century ago and the blacks of today is poverty *and* density.

The one statistical correlation that holds is the relationship of crime and violence to low income. To be sure, at any time and place the poor may be represented by one ethnic group. But over longer time spans and in various territories, violence and crime cross ethnic lines. Thus a century ago the trouble in Eastern-seaboard cities in America was laid at the feet of the Irish. Today it is supposedly the blacks and Puerto Ricans. In the American Southwest the Chicanos are held responsible. In the industrial urban centers of Germany, blame is directed at southern Europeans. The Japanese-American middle class of Hawaii see the poor Hawaiian as the source of crime. In Mexico the Ladinos, or middle-class segments of the Mexican population think the Indios, or the poorer Indian peoples of Mexico are the source of Mexico's crime statistics.

There is no easy way to find an answer to the question of violence, though some researchers have tried. Lorenz (1966) argues that aggression is a function of how close an animal is to the center of his territory when that territory is invaded. Conversely, he claims, the invading animal is less and less aggressive as he moves out of his own territory and enters the territory of another animal of the same species. This is why the small Chihuahua can often put a police dog to flight. It is not so simple with humans, however, and the popularizers, like Robert Ardrey (1966), of Lorenz's ideas do not add to our understanding of human behavior and in fact obscure the value of a territorial perspective.

Only when we can include the complexities and relativity of human behavior can we reach a hypothesis for humans similar to the one Lorenz concluded for animals. Like Lorenz, we could suggest that human aggression is a response to territorial invasion and hostility is the emotion of territorial disruption. But to understand the complexities of human behavior we would have to extend the concept of territoriality to include the territories discussed in this book as well as symbolic territories, such as the sphere of one's expertise, the rights of a speaker to the floor, cultural heterogeneity, or the economics of scarcity.

Very few of us have actually been involved in extreme kinds of violence. We have never been participants in or witnesses to homicide, a serious riot, or even a battlefield encounter. But all of us at one time or the other have been involved in what we might call situations of "mini-violence." A sharp exchange of words, a pushing or shoving contest, or an exchange of blows are events we've all more or less experienced. Suppose for the moment we return to some of the now familiar scenes of this book and give examples of incidents of mini-violence as pictured from a territorial perspective.

At Marblehead Beach the gradually increasing density of the afternoon eventually forced Tom's family to abandon this get-together, but not before some sharp words had been exchanged with intruding outsiders. At one point early in the day the children of Tom's family had accidentally let a ball roll into the central conversational space held by Tom and three other people. A young child had dashed into the center, retrieving the ball, but Tom and the other adults had treated the incident as the playful intrusion of a child. When an older boy chased after the ball, he paused just outside the group, waiting for Tom to retrieve the ball. Again this was treated as a minor intrusion and the appropriate and polite behavior of pausing defined the boundaries of the interruption.

By late afternoon, however, the situation had changed. The principal intrusions were made by outsiders who for one reason or the other violated the temporary territory claimed by Tom's family gathering. One child chased a ball into the group, colliding with an adult. Glares and scolding followed this violation. At another instance a child inadvertently kicked sand into Tom's cluster, precipitating a severe scolding from Tom. The frequency of violations in this partly-crowded public place elicited the behaviors of grumbling and overt hostility, attitudes the opposite of those exhibited earlier when territorial violations were less evident.

This is not to suggest that mini-violations did not occur within Tom's group, for they did. One mother continuously reprimanded her child for interrupting her conversation. At one point she slapped him for invading the picnic baskets. Once she shook him good for pouring sand on a younger sibling. Part of his problem seemed to focus on his repeated attempts to intrude on his mother's conversation space and consume her attention. One little two-year old was the constant target of abuse thrown at him by other children. He disrupted their play, destroyed their sand castles, and took toys that didn't belong to him. Another young girl sat between her father's legs and tried to ward off any child who approached her. She even screamed at the dog to get away when he approached to be petted. It looked as though she wanted to define an exclusive space for herself within the location held by her father.

On public conveyances conventionally polite behaviors usually serve their purpose, for most people respect claims for private spaces in public. Exceptions, however, do occur. On board a flight, for example, one fellow sitting next to a young couple very obviously had had too much to drink. At first the couple's defensive behaviors were the polite statements normally used by people who wish to be left alone. But on one or two occasions when the man leaned across her companion and spoke rudely to the woman, their behaviors immediately escalated into more hostile actions. They asked the fellow to cease disturbing them. He grumbled and withdrew for a moment, but then suddenly invited the other man to step into the aisle and settle the matter man to man. The stewardess approached the threesome, attempting to calm down what was by now a plane-wide ruckus. The man was standing and yelling at both the couple and the stewardess, when finally the co-pilot and several passengers bodily pushed him into a rear seat to calm down.

When people are packed together in rather narrow confines, as in the example of the delayed troop train, they become relatively motionless and take extra care of where they place their body parts, especially the hands. One fellow on the train disobeyed this rule and rather continuously touched his neighbor. The neighbor in turn squirmed visibly at the contact and tried to move away. We might say he was "touchy," but then people from some ethnic groups are very "touchy" and go to great lengths to avoid tactile contact and get quite upset if it does occur in public. The English, British-Americans, and Germans are examples. In contrast, other people are highly tactile. They rather continuously touch in public without embarrassment. Hispanic-Americans and peoples of Eastern European Jewish descent are examples. When the neighbor finally blew his top and threatened violence, his reaction seemed totally justified by some of the men and unjustified by others. Assigning blame in this case is what we Westerners usually do, but taking sides on blame issues hardly solves anything. This is a simple matter of different territorial rules or coding systems.

Other instances require different explanations. Not too long ago we witnessed a collision on the street. One fellow who was walking with his head down failed to take the evasive steps people use in high-density pedestrian traffic. He bumped into an oncoming woman and knocked some packages out of her arms. She glared and scolded him as he bent to help her pick up the packages. Our absentminded pedestrian apologized several times and then each proceeded on his way, terminating a brief intrusion. The territorial invasion could be placed squarely on his shoulders.

There are less unambiguous incidents, however. One man hurrying through a crowd might try to pass around a row of young men walking side by side in a phalanx. In so doing, what if he runs into another pedestrian trying to do the same from the opposite direction? Neither had a clear view. Neither was careless or inattentive. Some of us might want to direct the blame at the teen-agers who did not politely break ranks on a crowded sidewalk to accommodate other people. Yet Goodrich (1975) argues that pedestrians on crowded sidewalks in New York normally form columns of two or three in a line in each direction. A faster-moving pedestrian weaving in and out of these files can easily cause a collision. The moving order of the territorial formation is disrupted. Add to this very high densities with obstructions on the sidewalks, and progress will have to be negotiated with the consummate skill and maximum attention customarily given by the experienced Manhattanite.

One doesn't have to study the behavior of shoppers in, say, Filene's bargain basement in Boston to conclude that violations and confrontations are commonplace at such crowded sales counters. Film directors have occasionally captured this as comedy in the familiar scene of two women picking up the same garment at the same moment and then tearing it before either let it go. The altercation could be blamed on their stubbornness, but then there was marked ambiguity as to who had a claim on the garment. It belonged to neither of them, for the simultaneity of the claims precluded the use of the typical first-come, first-served American custom. Territorial ambiguity is a frequent source of violence.

In one family a little sister regularly taunted her four brothers into misdeeds. She would then tattle on them. For example, the boys were forbidden to play in the living room and the small kitchen was also off limits except at mealtimes. On one occasion the four brothers were in their usual locations in the hallway doing their homework. When anyone walked through the hallway, the boys were obliged to retract their legs to allow passage. They did so smartly when either parent walked past. The little sister began her usual taunting behavior by walking up and down the aisle over and over again, forcing the boys to move their legs each time she passed. Soon the boys stopped moving, but she just stepped over each pair of legs until she reached the other end. Then she turned and began the return course. On this trip, how- ever, one boy raised his leg just high enough at the right mo- ment to trip her. She started to fall, regained her balance, and then hit him. He jumped up and chased her into the living room.

The arrival of the screaming girl brought the matter to the parents' attention. As is customary for people in this society, the parents did not interpret this altercation in territorial terms, but instead sought the source of who was at fault. Somebody had to be the cause of all this uproar. The mother blamed the boy for picking on his little sister by trying to trip her. The father slapped him for coming into the living room when he had been explicitly told to stay out. One parent directed her anger at the boy's behavior toward his sister, the other at the boy's infraction of a parental rule. From our vantage point we witnessed one territorial violation being heaped upon another with a variety of defensive rules being in force. The final territorial intrusion was that of the slap, the father using this as a means of punishment for the other territorial violation of entering the parents' private space.

In one household we placed a television camera in the master bedroom, which in this family was the main congre- gating area. It was the central family room, and if we wanted to watch household members going about their daily tasks in the evening, we had to have a camera in a room that in other households would have been a more private area.

On evening after evening the parents would lie on the bed watching television and one child or the other would enter the room, get onto the bed, and cuddle with the parents and watch television for a time. The child would then move away and pursue another activity, sometimes even in the same room. The parents not only enjoyed these "intrusions" but openly encouraged them. In this family an otherwise rela- tively private space was also being treated as a communal space. Contrast this example with the previous illustration where even the normally communal living room was held as a private space for the parents. How different the territorial rules can be for the same kind of space even in the same cultural tradition!

In short, we have pictured the immediate contexts of mini-violence as cases where a clear intrusion is met by an active defense; cases where all parties share in the intrusion; those instances in which a set of reciprocal intrusions form actions and reactions in an escalating sequence; and episodes in which it is difficult to pinpoint the occurrence of an intrusion when there is a great deal of ambiguity concerning territorial boundaries or unexpected rules of privacy.

Now let us return to the violence that catches sensational attention. Once we leave the murky waters of blaming people, environments, and events, we find that violence readily falls within the same descriptive concepts of clear intrusion, mutual participation, escalation, and ambiguity.

A driver plows head on into an oncoming vehicle, injuring the other driver. He was clearly on the wrong side of the road. Legally he was at fault. Yet many would say he had little other choice if he had just swerved to avoid hitting a pedestrian who was invisible because he wore dark clothing on a dark night. A group of young men get into a fight in a bar and one man is accidentally shot. What were these men doing in the bar and why did one of them carry a gun?

Was violence intended? On questioning, we learn that these men had traveled into the neighborhood to attend a basketball game; and since two of them had been mugged in the neighborhood previously, one of them brought along a gun for protection. Following the excitement of a thrilling game, the men sought the conviviality of a bar, a location that thousands of men across this country visit nightly. Someone in the neighborhood bar had uttered a racial slur and one incident escalated into another.

There are places especially prone to the occurrence of violence. Some cities and towns rate major intersections in terms of the frequency of automobile accidents. The frequency of accidents at any given intersection especially in suburban and exurban communities will determine if a stop sign should be added at the intersection. Usually such places of high accident rates are marked by definite ambiguities as to right of way and difficulties in observing approaching traffic.

Despite the urbanite's fear of street muggings and the like, a very high percentage of violent crimes made against a person are committed inside the residence. There are rooms in the apartment and house that are likely to be places of violence. In the United States these are the kitchen and bedroom. Given the status structure between the sexes and the sexual division of labor, we could speculate that these are the two rooms of the house in which the territories are divided according to sex and in which territorial violations are most likely to occur. At the extreme, the higher crime rates in the bedroom are rape and assault either with guns, blunt instruments, cords, or fists. In the bedroom, men are more likely to be the aggressors and these are the characteristic means by which men of the household commit violence on the women of the household. In the kitchen, extreme forms of violence are likely to be carried out by women using knives or other sharp instruments or poison.

At the level of the apartment-house complex, the places where violence is most likely to occur include the stairs and fire escapes, elevators, some places in the lobby, and back fire doors that can be jammed open. These places are prone to high crime rates because they are poorly lit and, given most modern high-rise layouts, difficult to defend through surveillance. They are also the portions of the apartment house most commonly the routes of entry for intruders (Newman, 1972). Those areas under rather continual surveillance from the street, apartment-house building, or apartments have significantly lower crime rates.

At the level of the neighborhood, crimes are most likely to occur in public streets, alleyways, and places of public transportation. Vacant subway stops and exits are extremely hazardous at night. To reduce crime in these places, New York City, for example, has taken to closing down certain entrances and exits in the light traffic hours after dark. Similarly only the first few cars of a subway train are open to passen-

gers during late night and early morning hours, as police surveillance can easily monitor these cars. Crimes in the neighborhood also occur at those places frequented by the
underworld. Places of gambling, certain bars, houses of pros-
titution, etc., are more likely to be places with high crime
rates than will be the more residential and legitimate commercial areas of the neighborhood.

Finally, at the level of the town and city, Porterfield
(1965) argues that rates of violence for homicides and automobile accidents rise sharply in towns and cities characterized
by high heterogeneity of ethnic and class mix. This is true not
only for the United States but for the world as a whole. An
interesting side note to Porterfield's findings is that, even
though homicide increases with the level of cultural diversity,
the homicides are more likely to be committed on one's own.
Thus people are more likely to kill relatives, friends, ac-
quaintances, neighbors, and not to cross cultural lines to commit murder and mayhem.

Let us now try to develop a concept of violence that includes *both* the personality of those who are involved in violence *and* the situational and territorial conditions in which
violence occurs.

The first we might call running amok. At its least malignant
form, this kind of violence may involve nothing more than an
anxious, angry, or harassed person who drives much too fast
and carelessly. In its more detrimental forms a quiet young
man, long bound to his home by overdependency on a parent,
the type we previously described as locked into an unhealthy
one-to-one bond and an unusually confining territorial experience, at some trigger point breaks free, violating the territories of other people in a violent rampage. We find the common context for this type of violence as being a scarcity of
other affiliations and resources.

A second type of violence is that of taking advantage. An
individual who suffers from the extreme deprivations of poverty and lives in a context marked by scarcity of resources
and disintegration takes advantage of a situation in which a

territory is poorly bounded, inadequately kept under surveillance, and commits a crime against property and people. The immediate act of aggression is political-economic, but it is given a criminal label by the justice system and the wider society. Not labeled as criminal are the conditions under which the individual has been socialized, since he who takes advantage in this instance has already been taken advantage of. The violence is mutual. We believe the type of person living in this context who is most likely to commit a crime will have few associates outside a criminal element and will not have absorbed the cultural values of the other residents in his neighborhood.

The third kind of violence is violation with retaliation. One transgression feeds into another in a reciprocating relationship. A person found in an improper place for example, is accused of a territorial violation by a policeman or security guard, who, then, in turn, commits a violation of the person by touching and searching the individual. A neighbor encroaches on another's privacy or space and is rewarded with a retaliatory encroachment. Numerous comical examples illustrate this very point. Any number of films, television and radio shows have pictured the neighbor who attempts to retaliate with counternoise against the disturbing sounds made by the boy next door playing the trumpet, or the neighbor who telephones the people upstairs at 6 A.M. because they had a loud party until 3 A.M. Two nations may each encroach upon the other's air space and each may use the transgression as an excuse for another transgression or to justify another arms buildup of more sophisticated ways to commit further transgressions.

One common thread running through these three types is the feature of territorial disintegration. Boundaries are ambiguous, disputed, or poorly defended. Inequities of resources and scarcity of resources are likely to play a role as well. The inner turf may be insufficiently surveyed and monitored, and the jurisdiction may be confused and conflicting. And the occupants of this space will be inadequately linked to a network that includes friends and relatives; they will be of diverse cul-

tural or ethnic backgrounds; and, they will be openly hostile
to one another.

Territoriality has become a relatively popular subject, since
many people eagerly look for convenient handles through
which visible human behavior can be tied to the more nebulous realms of unconscious motivations and instinctual drives.
When research suggested that mankind shared similar territorial behaviors with other animals, the immediate popular response concluded that territoriality demonstrated the primacy
of instinct in human actions (Ardrey, 1966). Even such notable scholars as Tinbergen and Lorenz considered the weight
of evidence to favor instinct.

Our perspective is quite different. There is no need to make
the highly questionable jump from behavior to the fuzzy conceptions of hidden motivations and animal instincts. Territoriality is a convenient means to picture the organization of
human affairs as reflected directly by visible behaviors.

There is an old debate among many learned people about
whether humans are creatures principally motivated by instinct or whether they learn the major features of their conduct. On the one side is a picture of humans locked into an
immutable series of biological programs: programs that can
be used to explain just about every deed, every invention,
every event. The extreme proponents of this cause, such as the
Jensens and Schocklys, characterize humans as being born
into unequal gene pools that limit potential for psychological
and intellectual development. Just as dangerous, though less
extreme, are popularizers such as Robert Ardrey who weave
enticing tales of man's dependence on instinct. The opposite
position has been taken by some anthropologists and sociologists who believe human beings are shaped totally by their
social environment. From this perspective man acquires his
character as he grows up and lives among his own kind.

These arguments are spurious, for man is a biological animal. Yet, unlike other animals, humans have evolved a culture, a particular way of life, a history, a present, a future
that like a large overlay modifies, reworks, and subjugates
those biological forces commonly referred to as instincts. Hu-

mans are much more: they create symbolic representations by designing patterns of ideas and things that are not yet concrete. They can vary sounds, shapes, and conceptions of time. In short, both animals and humans act and interact. They move about. They cluster and disperse. Their activities are not random, but are patterned and ordered. Humans, however, have added the dimension of culture, symbols, ideas, and artifacts, which complicates any event, any activity by making it appear to be more complex. All too often, people have attempted to cope with this complexity by reducing, by isolating out certain pieces of the event. Territoriality is one intellectual tool that permits us to deal with complexity by describing behaviors as they occur in the context of space and time.

"Body language" is another subject popularly believed to be simply an unconscious revelation of an individual's inner feelings. Again our goal has been to offer another explanation, for we contend that through "body language" humans structure and regulate their activities. They do so in myriad ways that may or may not have any connection with their thinking or feelings.

The way people use space, how they position themselves in relationship to other people, and how people move their bodies and parts of their bodies can be linked under the common rubric of territorial behaviors. The relevance of culture or ethnicity, social class, time, situation, and place, in turn, explain differences in behaviors. Once considered relevant, they, in fact, help to demonstrate how regular and ordered human behavior actually is.

Thus, within a territorial perspective, otherwise unconscious and meaningless body movements can be understood for what they are: acts of privacy, rules of intrusion, and defensive maneuvers. Within a territorial framework, the rules governing how we use space and move our bodies can be connected to the otherwise unrelated rules governing the building of houses, apartments, neighborhoods, and cities. From a territorial perspective, crowding and urban decay are not separate from changes in the sizes of apartments, the use of that space, and changes in traditionally stable neighborhood borders.

And, finally, a territorial perspective helps us to understand the problems of violence, problems that are inextricably linked with scarcity of resources and disintegration of familiar neighborhoods.

NOTES

PREFACE

1 Scheflen, Adam Kendon, a psychologist, and other members of the research team in the Bronx had been at work attempting to understand just what human territoriality was. It was a new endeavor and many of their efforts were devoted to ground-breaking techniques, methods of analysis, and theory. For example, a large part of the early research utilized audiovisual equipment for collecting daily records of behavior in the home. Such research techniques had not been attempted before at this level of complexity, and the problems with equipment coupled with the political repercussions and antagonisms toward this type of research and the very real concern of the researchers to protect the people volunteering to participate nearly lead to a total research disaster. All this occurred during those highly volatile years of 1968, 1969, and 1970. Nevertheless, Joseph Schaeffer, a young anthropologist, and Roy Loe, a cinematographer, collected a wealth of information These records provide a natural history account of individual families interacting among themselves and using their living space on a daily basis. Roy Loe also filmed people moving through public spaces in several cities around the world. Ashcraft later added to this by taking similar films in some detail in Rome, Munich, and the Bronx. Based on analysis of this data, Kendon and Scheflen, with the help of the research team, began to formulate a theory of human territoriality. Scheflen's schema and ideas appear in Scheflen with Ashcraft, 1975. After Ashcraft joined the research team, the effort broadened to examine behavior within the neighborhood, especially use of streets and other public places and a delineation of neighborhood borders.

2 Knowledge of territorial behavior seems to be learned by experience without the necessary intercession of consciousness and language, for people establish the same territorial manifestations over and over and they automatically obey the usual conventions of territorial usage and passage without knowing this consciously. Since this knowledge is trans-

mitted from generation to generation, we can also say that it is cultural just as a people's conceptions of territory are cultural. But to claim that the transmission of territorial order is cultural does not deny genetic transmission or neglect the role of physical environments. On the contrary, a cultural tradition integrates genetic and environmental determinants in its evolution. The various explanatory principles are complementary in a holistic explanation of this behavioral order. To say that a territorial order is culturally transmitted assumes then that the members of a tradition learn, carry cognitive images, and make plans in that order. These orders vary in accordance with values, options in the use of available space, innovations in arrangements, and emotional responses to ecological disruptions. What we are trying to avoid is a linear explanation that might indicate that each person invents territory for himself or that values or instincts *cause* these systems.

We have long held that in order to understand appreciably the meaning of human actions, we must observe people in the theater of their daily lives. Observation that is confined to some ideal laboratory conditions limits, distorts, and frequently offers a false interpretation of human behavior. In isolating variables, researchers have thought to mimic the so-called hard sciences of physics and chemistry by reducing complexity. But in so doing they destroy the very context in which a behavior occurs. And it is in this context that a human act has its meaning. What does it mean to say that smiling occurs all over the world? When, how, at which time, in what situations?

It is rather like saying that every human experiences the hunger drive. Not all people get hungry at the same time, nor under the same conditions. What will satisfy the appetite of a Malay fisherman will not do the same for a Bavarian hop farmer. Many of us know the story that an Irishman has not had a sufficient meal until he has eaten a potato. The same story in Bengal would be rice. The American lost in a tropical rain forest may starve because he does not know what is edible. Some people's stomach turns at the thought of culturing yogurt with cow's urine, eating raw fish, having oysters on the half shell, or ordering a peppermint and caramel sundae topped with marshmallow flavoring. Hunger is relative, and so is smiling.

People don't live under laboratory conditions. They live in the richness of everyday experience, and it is in this complexity that we find meaning for their behaviors.

CHAPTER 1: TERRITORIES

1 Until a few years ago, little attention was given to men's territorial behavior. Nevertheless, studies of a territorial dimension were occurring (Howard, 1920; Lorenz, 1952, 1966; Vine, 1973; Watson, 1924), and they gradually built to a climax, catapulting the concept into the public's attention (Robert Ardrey's popular *The Territorial Imperative* [1966] and Konrad Lorenz and Tinbergen recently being awarded the Nobel Prize). Needless to say, once a concept gains acceptability, it is frequently used and misused by those who wish to jump on the scientific bandwagon and ride whatever is in vogue. Many people were

probably influenced by Ardrey's popular account to suppose that a territory is nothing more than a piece of turf carved out by a species solely
on the basis of instinct. Whatever value this notion may hold for others,
it does not represent the one we shall discuss in this book.

2 To view the world as if it is made up of organic and physical objects
provides us with one kind of picture. Thus, the fixed territory must be
located somewhere, a somewhere marked by topographical features or
by its relationship to other territories in the region. Consequently, the
territory of one animal or group of animals lies among the territories of
others of that species. Part of the environment then becomes a system
of other and like territories. Territory as a physical object is also a habitat, a system of geophysical, climatological, and social relationships.

In many species of animals the boundaries of a fixed or stationary
territory will be marked in some discernible way. Some animals urinate
or defecate around the perimeters of a stationary parcel of space and
members of that species apparently recognize the smell and react to it
as warnings of a territorial border. Deer bite the bark from the trees
around the perimeter. Man, too, constructs visible lines such as fences
or walls.

Often those who hold a territory tend to reside toward its geographic
center, leaving a buffer zone of space at the peripheries. When animals
or people are assembled in a place, newcomers or strangers tend to
pass around, giving them a respectable berth. If they do not, those who
occupy the place may threaten or even attack them. They may display
their canines in the characteristic baboon yawn, bite the air, beat their
breasts, growl, and even make mock rushes at the outsiders who approach them. These have been referred to as "territorial defense behaviors" in ethology.

3 A similar problem of definition emerges with respect to moving territories. If a person leaves place *A* and proceeds to place *B*, we may assume that he is moving from one territory to another. But our assumption would be based on the concrete locations and less on the behavior.
What of the territory created by his movement? He claims a space
through which he moves, and that space is defined not just by the physical features of body size, but also by conventions, culture, density, and
location. Ordinarily, respect is given to a region around the path of
movement, just as respect is given to a region around a stationary location.

The spatial dimensions and the location of a territory, then, are relative. They are relative to the context of the situation. Boundaries and
defense behaviors hold for an interval of time. Then they change. A
particular parcel of space may be treated as a territory by one group in
a particular tradition in a given species. But that region of space may
not be, and usually is not, a territory to those of another tradition or
species. Hence, a claim to a given space cannot be a territory if that
claim is not respected.

4 An event does not occur in isolation. It occurs in relation to other
events. How we see these events as being put together marks our epis-
temology. In this book, we do not consider that at one side stands the
individual and at the other his environment. Our language forces us to
separate subject from object, but the field approach enables us to put
them together in relational terms. A room lies within a house, which
lies within a block, and so on. In this sense, the room does not have as

its environment the house, the block, etc; instead, the room is defined by its relation within the house. The house is a next level of complexity, or a *context* for the room. We are interested in how people use the room and how the flow of events in room use characterize the room in relation to its position to other rooms and to the dwelling as a whole.

Context is not just environment. It is the next level of complexity in which the behavior is embedded. The contexts of a personal space are systems of interpersonal space, in a particular activity, in some cultural tradition of activities, and within the total system of activities of man. Context is simply a term used to relate an event's occurrences to the situation and time in which that event occurs. To put it in other terms, an event occurs within the jurisdiction and aegis of some social and cultural system larger than the event itself.

CHAPTER 2: PRIVACY

[1] As far as space is concerned, they acted as a social unit. They engaged in other behaviors as well, which defined them as a pair, or what Goffman (1971) refers to as statements that they were "with" each other. They held identical postures, were oriented in the same direction, held a similar eye focus, and co-acted with similar rhythm in speaking and gesticulating. And, while Tom's location was private to him, a location of similar space was not private to each of them, but to both of them as a unit. (It could be argued that each held a smaller private personal space, but in relation to Tom and to the conversational unit as a whole, they clearly acted as an identifiable subunit.) Since privacy is relative to one's place in a cluster of locations, we can say that the couple was less private vis-à-vis each other, but as a unit more private vis-à-vis Tom.

[2] We can note by these behaviors that people who are engaged in a face-to-face conversation have defined a private space which others outside the group are expected to respect. Outsiders observe this by not hearing or pretending not to hear what is being said, by not looking into the space, and by avoiding the space in passing or by standing at an imaginary boundary awaiting an invitation to enter the group.

[3] Scheflen with Ashcraft (1975) refer to this open area as the space of orientation.

[4] Compare other examples of enclosed territories. In churches, for instance, there are relatively fixed locations assigned to the type of participant. There is a region for the choir, a region for the congregation, and a region for the minister and his aides. Normally the leader of the ceremony has several locations he uses at different points in the ritual: there is the chancel, a spot in back of the pulpit, the pulpit itself, and the rectory.

The stadium or arena is similar to but contrasts with the arrangement in the church. In the stadium there is a central court or arena that is reserved for the active players. Certain supportive personnel, such as substitutes, trainers, and team physicians, may enter the playing field with permission. Others, such as coaches and management, may not. Around the nucleus of the playing field is a region for the supportive personnel. On the periphery are the rings of spectators. Still farther to the periphery are auxiliary places such as hot-dog stands, ticket booths, guard areas, rest rooms, etc. There are at least four concentric rings of space that comprise the territory of the stadium. Each zone has its own rules of penetration and privacy. Spectators may not enter the playing area during the performance. Similarly players may not enter the spectators' zone. Few of these zones are private from gaze and sound. Areas such as the locker and shower rooms, ticket booths, management offices, and police control offices are, however, defined more privately.

CHAPTER 3: INTRUSIONS

1 Our principal means of collecting data was based on filming with Super 8 mm and 16 mm cameras pedestrian traffic in New York, Philadelphia, San Francisco, London, Munich, Rome, Paris, and Moscow.

2 Thus the matter of intrusion is relative to the social relationships of those who occupy adjoining spaces and to the activities in which they are engaged. The problem in research, moreover, is that it is difficult to distinguish the intrusions of voice, gaze, and gesticulation from the intrusions of movement into private space, since moving into the space occupied by another person or group of people often accompanies looking and talking into that private space.

3 A major portion of our research interest over the past few years concerned studying the system of privacy and intrusion within the household. We have long been suspicious of what people tell researchers and we know the limitations of questionnaires from personal experience. We prefer instead to observe the daily activities of people firsthand. We did bolster our ethnographic observations with interviews, the administration of questionnaires to a larger sample of the population, and demographic studies. The main thrust of our research in the home, however, focused on the intensive observation of a few families.

Ethnographers customarily move into a community and, through a process of some participation in people's activities and long-term observation, attempt to build a picture of the local way of life. Ideally the anthropologist prefers to remain with the population for a period of a year or two. In small rural hamlets or moderately populated regions he is usually successful in accounting for the main features of local daily life. In crowded urban neighborhoods, however, the problem of capturing details is almost insurmountable.

To provide the depth of observation we desired, we asked a number of families in the Bronx to participate in our study by allowing us to place three television cameras in their apartment. We located one camera in the living room, one in the hallway, and one in the kitchen. Since a videotape camera is noiseless and has no disturbing lights, the intrusion of the camera as a foreign object high on the wall was minimal. In those households which we studied on a long-term basis, for weeks, and months, we rented a vacant apartment nearby to set up the monitoring equipment. In this instance we controlled the monitor and we usually let it run from very early morning until late into the night.

For those families where the camera was left for shorter periods, we located a portable set complete with monitor in the home itself. We placed the cameras at the desired location, instructed the adults in the operation of the equipment, indicated the kinds of family gatherings we were especially interested in, and asked them to make us a family documentary. They could turn the equipment on and off as they wished, for the monitoring equipment was under their control.

We were very aware of the intrusion of the camera and we momentarily compensated those families who agreed to participate in our research. But we felt more of an obligation. First of all each family reviewed the tape and could erase what they did not wish to be preserved. Families may not want squabbles or other information held on a public tape, however confidential the research and storage of information may be. For our purposes we would lose no valuable information, anyway, as we wanted a long-term daily account, not individual incidents. To our surprise, not one family ever chose to erase a tape. Secondly, since most of our families were from the poorer sections of the Bronx ghetto, we took on the obligation of helping them through the interface of minority person versus government bureaucracy. Thirdly, we made a concerted effort to feed back what we were learning into the neighborhoods of the Bronx. We argued for and helped foster a program of community psychiatry. We met with local leaders and attended neighborhood meetings.

4 A role is not just a fixed set of behaviors performed by a single individual. The activities humans perform in fulfilling the demands of a particular role function within a set of contexts, the most visible of which would be the immediate context of the situation. The role we call mothering, for instance, should be considered as a system of behaviors that are played out in a particular situation. In any introductory sociology textbooks, students are led to believe that mothering as a role functions as a result of a series of trait lists offered by an author. Within a territorial framework, however, the role of mother, or what we are here calling mothering, is not a list of activities, but instead particular behaviors which occur within particular spatial-temporal contexts. That is, in seeing behavior as territorial we notice that certain spatial locations will be assigned to certain roles under certain conditions at certain times.

5 In relating examples we run the risk that the illustrations will either confirm previous prejudices or seem cute, but hardly relevant to the larger issues of mankind.

We found this general danger even in our own research team. Some members expected, for instance, to witness endless battles among the children for a favorite chair or other special location in the living room. When there weren't sufficient chairs at the kitchen table, many of us expected quarrels over who would eat first, and so on. When these expectations didn't appear, there was some surprise. And as we all watched Puerto Rican and black American siblings live together day after day without doing battle, there was a general feeling among us of how lovely these children were. Puerto Rican children would sit for hours crowded two and three into a single chair in front of the TV set without a single argument or skirmish. We could observe no cross-gender rivalry among Puerto Rican children either, even though we watched them daily for months on end. Such observations should force all of us to revise our predilections concerning what is normal.

Among the black families we sampled, children tended to ignore television even though the set was on from morning into night. Their play consisted of milling about the room without sitting and directly watching TV and without much use of objects. They focused on inter- personal relationships in some game, mock fighting, comparing size, etc. There was much less task orientation than among white middle-class children. Black siblings of the same sex rarely argued, and we never witnessed a single altercation. What we did observe was an incredible amount of caretaking among the children.

We recall many instances of an older brother without request sharing his food with his next younger brother. Similarly girls shared their pos- sessions readily with younger sisters. This was done with or without adults present. In fact, in our sample, adults were frequently absent, ei- ther from the apartment or from the room. Consequently, the children were freely servicing one another without direct or continued prompting by adults. In the black households we also never witnessed one boy at- tempting to gain parental attention at the expense of a brother. An in- teresting example of how foreign this behavior is to the middle class recently occurred during a television interview. A white interviewer was questioning the small children of the singing group, the Jackson Five. So insistent was he on building the notion of sibling rivalry that he ap- parently failed to believe the boys when they claimed they did not argue with one another or compete over objects or people. In the inter- viewer's eyes, sibling competition was a normal, healthy behavior com- mon to all children. He thought the children were concealing some- thing and kept probing with one leading question after the other, much the same as a psychiatrist probes under the so-called defenses of his pa- tient.

Though boys do not quarrel or compete much with one another, nor do the girls with one another, we did observe frequent cross-gender ri- valry in black households. In one family this almost developed into a pathetic daily ritual. The little sister would tattle to her father about the various activities of her elder brothers. The father would then take out his strap and administer a harsh discipline to the boys on the basis of the sister's tales. She did not tell on her fellow sister, only on her brothers. The basis for many beatings rested on the family rule forbid- ding the children to use the living room when the parents were not at home. Of course the children did, and the littlest sister regularly re- ported to her father what the *boys* had done. The sister would intrude on the boys in other ways as well. Whenever the boys played on the floor with objects, she was likely to dash through the middle of their play, knocking over any assemblies. The boys would then chase and hit her. And as soon as father came home, this, too, was gladly reported.

6 Certain countries are more prone to invasions than others. England has been invaded only a few times in its history, while the countries of Central Europe and the Levant have been crisscrossed by invading ar- mies almost continuously. Poland, for example, ceased to exist as a na- tional territory on four occasions in the last two hundred years. Ger- mans, on the other hand, have been invaders of other territories on three major occasions in the last hundred years. Obviously the propen- sity and the frequency of invasion have had something to do with topographical barriers. The countries of Central Europe, for instance, are divided by political barriers. There are not large bodies of water or high mountain chains that divide these territories.

CHAPTER 4: DEFENSE

1 Defense behavior tells us what the territory is for those animals without a clearly visible boundary, such as a wall or fence might be. A defensive maneuver might include simply an attempt to maintain a fixed distance; that is, on threat of an intrusion, an animal or person may simply back off, relinquishing a piece of ground but continuing to maintain a particular distance of space between the intruder and defender. If we see territory as a parcel of ground, we have witnessed a conquest and a yielding. But if we conceive of a territory as a behavioral space, then the maneuver can be interpreted as a successful defense of interpersonal distance, of *a* space not a piece of ground. The animal's defense has not been marked by a recourse to violence or active threat.

CHAPTER 5: CONSTRAINTS

1 There is the frightening possibility that human psychology could be used in the interests of social engineering to persuade people to "feel" they have enough space even when that space is insufficient. Unfortunately this process is already under way. Builders of office space or the new high-rise apartment buildings use every possible gimmick, including on occasions out-and-out criminal activity, to persuade, induce, or force people to abandon their dwellings to the construction ball. We continually run the risk of being offered the illusion that the new spaces will be better and more comfortable.

CHAPTER 7: SCARCITY

1 Cf. Liebow's study of Washington, D.C., as compared with our own studies of the Bronx.

APPENDICES

APPENDIX A

Within a field or systems way of seeing, particular units are inextricably embedded in a web of other units so that any particular unit of behavior gains meaning only when examined against the passage in which it occurs. This is why we argue for a contextual analysis. As each element lies within a passage, so does the passage become an element in some larger or more complex passage. Consequently, contextual elements are organized in a hierarchical pattern of increasing complexity. The term hierarchy here has nothing to do with levels of power as we are prone to speak of a hierarchy of statuses or control. A unit of space can no longer be treated as if it is isolated, for we now recognize that it is but a subpart of a larger interdependent field.

As there is an almost infinite range of possible human spaces, we must make some effort to find at least a crude scheme for describing the various levels in the hierarchy of territorial organization. To this end, we find a division occurring between privately owned space, which we call *properties,* and publicly owned or governmental controlled spaces, which we call *land divisions.* Property is an area of space owned or controlled by a person or group of people such as the family, partnership, corporation, etc. It includes land, houses, office buildings, clubs, places of business, and so on. The neighborhood, town, city, state, nation-state are examples of territorial land divisions, or political units that have evolved in the course of human development.

Obviously there is some degree of overlap. The private properties of a corporation, for example, are not only larger than some neighborhoods and some nation-states but also extend their aegis over broader territorial spaces than just the spaces occupied by their properties. Nevertheless, we find it convenient to characterize levels of territories as properties and land divisions as outlined below (Scheflen with Ashcraft, 1975):

Level I (Property)

Level IA (Area)
Within the broader level of property we can describe a subunit of space we have called an area. It is small enough in size to include a group of one, two, or at most a dozen people who gather within the space and yet remain in direct contact with one another. They can touch and engage in interaction at small interpersonal distances such as intimate conversation or courtship. An example of a built space in the magnitude of the area would be the traditional domestic room, the living room, dining room, kitchen, or bedroom. Immediately we are struck by the observation that these built areas are specialized rooms used for different purposes, but that they do not exist in isolation but combine to form a base of operations for the social unit.

Level IB (Base)
We call the collective constellation of areas the base. In addition to the house or apartment, examples would include the combined rooms of a small department store, a small industrial plant, the local bar and restaurant, and the social club. The house, for instance, is a configuration of rooms or areas that in concert form a base of operations for the domestic unit.

Level IC (Complex or Compound)
The complex or compound is a configuration identifiable by having multiple bases of operation on the same property. The apartment house, with its many apartments and the supplementary space for storage, boiler rooms, mailrooms, lobby, etc., is an example. The palace, with its nuclear residence for the royal family and its surrounding bases for housing servants, the court, stables, and storage zones, would be another example. So would the military camp, which is in some ways analogous to the old fortified castle. The large department store with its multiple subdepartments, each with many areas, is yet another example of the complex.

Level ID (Division)
The concept of a division is used to include highly complex properties owned by a single institution, such as a corporation, but not necessarily constructed on the same grounds. The division, then, will consist of many subproperties such as mines, plants, or

agricultural holdings as well as office buildings, including the main administrative center and a network of branch offices that exist in many cities, states, and nations.

We can similarly divide governmental or land divisions along a four-level subdivision schema.

Level II (Land Divisions)

Level IIA (Locale or Neighborhood)
Included at this level would be the block, possibly in some instances the housing tract, and the village or urban neighborhood.

Level IIB (The Town)
This is a land division equivalent in size to the town in many parts of the United States.

Level IIC (The City or County)
Level IIC is a unit of governmental division approximately the magnitude of a city, or in the United States also of a county.

Level IID (The State)
This is a more complex configuration of bounded space that would include the region, state, nation, or even the continent.

The same general configuration of built space appears at one level of organization after another. The room layout has a nucleus containing tables and chairs and a region for storage and passage. The dwelling has a nucleus consisting of interconnecting rooms such as the living room and dining room and a region consisting of sleeping rooms, baths, work spaces, and storage areas. The complex has a nuclear area of offices, lobbies, and possibly shops and a region consisting of apartments. Similarly the neighborhood and the city may have a nuclear zone of public buildings and shops, a region of residential blocks, and a "surround" of industrial or open spaces.

Consequently, we can use the same terms at each level of organization to designate the subdivisions of a territory. For example:

Location (L)—in an area (Level IA), the location is a space ordinarily used or occupied by one person. At the level of the base (Level IB), the location becomes a particular room in a house. At the level of the complex (Level IC), the location becomes any base, any particular apartment in an apartment house or any particular house in a suburban housing development. And at the level of the division (Level ID), the location is any particular property lying within the large variegated institution.

At the level of land divisions, the location would be any particular block (Level II) lying within the neighborhood (Level IIA).

And at the level of the town (Level IIB), the location becomes any particular neighborhood in the town. At the level of the city (Level IIC), the location would be any particular political subdivision, such as a municipality, borough, or any particular complex of neighborhoods that have at least vague boundaries and a name—for example, downtown, East Side, West Side, the Upper West Side, etc. In the United States the political subdivisions of the county would include locations of the magnitude of towns and townships. Finally, we could include cities or counties as locations themselves at the level of larger political divisions (Level IID), such as the state.

Let us pause for a moment lest we lose sight of the forest for studying the trees. While we can note some exceptions, the magnitude of one subunit in the schema will combine with other similar units to form a larger or more inclusive sublevel, and so on. We are not just naming and classifying territories. More importantly, we are here schematically describing the order or possible contexts for behaviors that occur at one level of organization.

Just as a city is not a tree, so is the organizational hierarchy or territories not a unilinear model. There are several combinational possibilities, for the pattern is similar to the organizational model of the atom. A hydrogen atom, for instance, can double itself and become a hydrogen molecule (the base at Level IB can form part of a complex at Level IC, as is the case of the apartments in an apartment building or the house in some housing tracts). Or the hydrogen atom can combine with other atoms, forming a familiar compound of 2 hydrogen atoms and 1 atom of oxygen (or the base, Level IB, the house for instance, can form part of a block or neighborhood at Level IIA). The concept of a location (L), for example, provides us with an analytical means of understanding interdependencies of the parts, which is how the levels fit together in a hierarchical arrangement.

Module (M)—a subunit we code with the letter M. In any structure of human space it is unlikely that a single location will define a total area. Instead the space is likely to be fitted with a series of adjacent locations, such as a row of seats facing the stage, a row of rooms opening onto the same corridor in a public building, a row of houses on a block, or a set of adjacent neighborhoods or towns lying next to each other along a railroad or river. We call any cluster of side-by-side locations that face in the same direction a module (M). The important characteristic of a module, whether it includes a three-location or three-seated sofa or a row of four chairs on one side of a dining room table, is that the locations of the module all face the same direction.

Nucleus (N)—a unit more complicated than the location or module, which we code with the letter N. Locations and modules often face each other in architectural arrangements. Thus in the living room two modules, the seats of two sofas, may face each other across a coffee table. A chair comprising a single location may also be placed at either end of this cluster, forming a square in which the locations and modules all face into one another. In the living room, then, this nucleus or central cluster will comprise a complex of locations and modules of chairs, sofas, tables, TV sets, etc. In the dining room the nucleus is outfitted with a set of chairs or locations facing one another across the dining table.

The same configuration can also appear at more complex levels of organization, such as a row of rooms facing one another across a hall. In many standard office buildings we are confronted with a module of several offices lying on one side of a corridor facing a duplicate model on the other. A series of buildings may form part of a college campus by facing one another across an open quad. Rows of buildings may face one another across the commons in a colonial American town. We are all familiar with the main street of many towns and cities, with commercial establishments lining each side of the street. Similarly residential neighborhoods may lie next to each other in a town and bounding the central nucleus of commercial and public buildings of the town square. With an aerial view of the cluster, we would notice that the neighborhoods are multiple modules facing one another around the square. We call this kind of spatial arrangement, in which a cluster of locations and modules face one another, a nucleus and also claim that it exists at all levels of territorial organization.

It is also possible to have multiple nuclei, as is the case in a large city. In a city like New York, for instance, there are a number of nuclear zones. In Manhattan there is a zone for shopping— midtown; a zone for commercial activity—downtown; and a zone for entertainment—the Broadway area.

There are, however, other ways to arrange locations and modules. They can be stacked as multiple stories of the apartment house or office building instead of being clustered around a central nucleus. At each level of spatial organization, then, man has successively invented other ways to cluster locations and modules. Each of these has accommodated, yet also permitted, an extensive population increase and therefore an even higher density of people in a given space.[1]

APPENDIX B

One murky area that must be avoided is making generalizations about space requirements according to the number of people per

[1] We have been deliberately sketchy here concerning the organization of territorial levels, as we have treated the subject much more extensively elsewhere (Scheflen with Ashcraft, 1975).

hundred square feet or per acre. We've come across some building codes, for instance, prescribing that each child in a household shall have 60 square feet of living space. What sort of bureaucratic nonsense leads human beings to come up with such figures? Somehow there is an assumption that people endlessly stand in formations of one kind or another. It is rather like imagining human movement as the prancing of formations across a military parade field. Shades of Lieutenant Scheisskopf of *Catch 22*, who wanted to improve parade drill by bolting the arms of soldiers to their hips.

If a child supposedly requires 60 feet of living space, we might ask living space for what? Is this solely bedroom space where he deposits his body at night and his clothing around the clock? Or is this space in the kitchen or dining area for his use when eating? Or the living-room space he must use for play and watching television? Or the space in the bathroom he must use for ablutions and elimination? Or is it the space he must use as transit from room to room? The question is; how much space does a child require for which activities, at what times of the day, in which portions of the household, and in which portions of the neighborhood that supports the living space within the confines of the household? One of the first steps involved in trying to understand human space requirements is to go where humans carry out an activity and observe their behavior directly.

In the past, architects and designers have ignored public opinion and have laid out space according to principles operating in the profession. Recently, however, innovations in design inputs have attempted to involve clients. New experimental approaches to some extent rely on visits to a building site and interviewing clients before the project is crystallized into a room or building. The problem with this method is that relying exclusively on interviews almost virtually guarantees continuation of present ignorance.

Interviewing techniques may be appropriate for the psychological sciences and public opinion polls, where attitudes and values are the focus of concern. But public opinion of territorial issues is limited. People may be relatively aware of how they feel about various matters that are part of the public's conscious awareness. But what does it mean to claim that a certain percentage of Americans think that Gerald Ford is not performing well in office? For lack of another indicator, some of us accept this as a measure of how Americans would vote. When it comes to asking people to participate in a description of something that is not in the public's consciousness, we tread on even thinner ice.

If people are questioned about the grammar of their speech, they would probably respond with something like nouns, objects, indirect objects, and transitive and intransitive verbs, for this is what they have learned in grammar school. They are unaware of the process by which sounds are put together and how lexical units build a structure forming the English language. Public opinion would be useless to the linguist, who uses informants only as speakers of the language. He would build his own model of sounds and grammar and then check his hypothesis with the native informants to see if a particular utterance sounded correct. So must it also be with territorial issues.

People do not know how they use space. Asking them about space will simply call up the learned clichés and habits of how to answer such questions. This lack of public knowledge about space use is not the consequence of human stupidity, but instead the results of a long process of indoctrination. For generations people have had to live with and learn to live in spaces allotted to them on the basis of either traditional values or economic and profit-oriented motives. In the United States peoples from Southern and Eastern Europe, Africa, and Latin America have had to live in spaces built for the most part on the traditions of England and Northern Europe. Not only that, but they have also had to adapt to space allocations divided and subdivided according to class values. To expect these peoples to understand the forces at work in building their dwelling spaces or to appreciate the nature of their own space requirements is like asking the ivory-tower cynic to reform and expand his own sophistry.

Americans have been taught to pay attention to decor, aesthetics, and economics. They are accustomed to articulating their grievances as well as their wishes within this very limited framework of space use. Thus residents of working-class or ghetto apartments on being interviewed complain about the discrepancies between their apartments and those of the middle or wealthier classes. They are not in a position to discuss layout and room design in any way that would yield a meaningful input to design or reform architecture. Similarly generations of Americans in all classes have been bombarded with values of furniture size and design. It would be a gross injustice to aspirations, aspirations instilled by advertising the American style, to turn around now and suggest to poorer urban residents that middle-class sized furniture is far too bulky and impractical for the floor space in their apartments.

Any interviewing for opinions about space, therefore, must be bolstered by a heavy reliance on how people actually use the space they have. We must get away from basing our conclusions on how people imagine they use their space. Videotape or motion-picture films provide us with one kind of opportunity to gain an empirical yet direct understanding of how people use space. We cannot claim that interpreting the results will be simple. It certainly offers no panacea, but it does get us away from imagination and returns us to use.

If we find, as we did in our research in the Bronx, that Puerto Ricans, for example, tend to use only one portion of the living room during the evening and for all practical purposes make little use of other apartment spaces, are we then to conclude that Puerto Rican families might require even less space, as one New York City planner concluded? Like the 60 square-foot space allotment for children, such conclusions assume that the space required is that actually occupied by the physical body. Our own research blunders taught us very well that unoccupied space is as intimately critical to use as the space actually occupied by the human body. Moreover, a space not used at one time of the day during a particular activity may be tensely critical at another point of time during another activity. Thus to tamper with unoccupied space is potentially to tamper with the functioning of the organism.

How people fill a space with furniture or other objects is also linked to space use. As we enter the ghetto apartment of a black American family, we might find, again as we discovered on more than one occasion, that the physical space as used is too small to provide seating for all family members in either kitchen or living room. Located in one corner may be large objects never used by the family. This could be a piano that no one can play or two overly large TV and hi-fi consoles, one of which has not functioned for some time. We might quickly offer an extremely perceptive recommendation: this "junk" ought to be removed from the apartment. But the householder protests.

Where would he move this "junk" to? Any communal storage space in the basement is totally untrustworthy, for anything of value will be stolen immediately. Unlike the upper middle class, he has no funds to pay for storage. Well, then, just throw the stuff out. If he cannot afford to pay to have it carted away, then call the city sanitation department to pick it up off the sidewalk. Yet the householder's hesitation could be the result of other more intrinsic factors. The broken piano may belong to a brother who does not have an apartment of his own. The family is keeping this man's cherished possession. It is not just a junk object, but a symbol of one man's ambition or urge to have some diversion in an otherwise closed and negative universe. The family is holding the piano for a future date, a date that may never arrive in reality. In another circumstance, the piano and consoles might be the one set of middle-class symbols separating this family in their minds from other ghetto residents. It is their belief in an eventual escape from the slums. These objects, then, are not just takers of space; they are dynamically involved in what is "living" to a particular household.

Looking at space use rather than speculating about its use raises a host of other questions. What if we do determine the traditional living space of Puerto Ricans, Dominicans, or Cubans? Are they then to be condemned to traditionalism by transposing this customary space to North American urban centers? Would they be inhibited from merging into the mainstream of American life, and would segregation instead of integration be the result? But by disrupting tradition and forcing Americanization, we also run the risk of homogenizing society, of standardizing values, aspirations, and world views, of perpetuating discrimination, poverty, and even violence. The questions may not have solutions.

It may be a blessing in disguise that we do not have a set of idealized and accepted norms for space as we have had imposed on us for mental health, nutrition, intelligence, and competence. If we did, we would probably also impose artificial, class-bound, and ethnocentric standards upon human living conditions. To a large extent, this already occurs, though it may be partly unwitting. Traditional British-American space increments described earlier in some measure act as standards in the design of living space throughout this country.

How much nuclear space will be required depends on what sort of regional and "surround" space is readily available. How much of any of these space layouts is required also depends on the type of activities that will occur within them, the duration of the activity, how many participants are involved, how long the participants will be confined to the space, and how much freedom they have to leave and return. Still further, space requirements depend on lighting, air circulation, decor, the absence or presence of windows, and so on. In view of the multiple systems of contexts that exist within any empirically sound notion of space requirements, it is unlikely that any single solution will emerge.

We might profit from previous construction of dwelling space by checking back for adequacy and resources. It might also be possible to build a model mock-up to find out how it will be used before it is finally and permanently constructed—a similar notion was employed at some colleges in the layout of lawns, hedges, and pathways. Students used the open spaces for a period of time and then, once it was learned what the transit paths were in actuality, landscaping began. A more practical technique in architecture is the building of high-variability architecture in which subunits vary in layout and size and do not conform to some standard module.

REFERENCES

Adorno, T. W., Frenkel-Brunswick, E., Levinson, D. J., Sandford, R. N. *The Authoritarian Personality*. New York: Harper, 1950.

Ardrey, Robert, *The Territorial Imperative: A Personal Inquiry into the Animal Origins of Property and Nations*. New York: Dell Publishing Co., 1966.

Ashcraft, Norman. *Colonialism and Underdevelopment: The Processes of Political Economic Change in British Honduras*. New York: Teachers College Press, 1973.

Bateson, Gregory. "The Message 'This Is Play'" Schaffner, Bertram, (ed.), *Group Processes; Transactions of the Second Conference* (held 9–12 October 1955 at Princeton, New Jersey). New York: Josiah Macy, Jr. Foundation, 1955, pp. 145–242.

Bell, Daniel. "Notes on the Post-Industrial Society" in *The Public Interest*. Copyright National Affairs, Inc., 1967.

Calhoun, J. B. "Population Density and Social Pathology," *Scientific American*, 206, 1962, pp. 139–48.

Castaneda, Carlos. *The Teachings of Don Juan: A Yaqui Way of Knowledge*. New York: Ballantine Books, 1968.

Christian, J. J. "Adrenal and Reproductive Responses to Population Size in Mice," *Ecology*, 37, 1956, pp. 258–73.

Davis, Kingsley. "Population Policy: Will Current Programs Succeed?" *Science*, 158, Oct./Nov. 1967, p. 730.

Freedman, J. L. *Crowding and Behavior*. New York: The Viking Press, 1975.

Goffman, Erving. *Behavior in Public Places*. New York: The Free Press, 1963.

Goffman, Erving. *Relations in Public*. New York: Basic Books, 1971.

Goodrich, Ronald. "A Study of Co-active Crowding Streets, Its Effects on Privacy Seeking, and Its Reduction by One's Experience of Perceived Control." Unpublished Manuscript, 1974. New York City University Environmental Psychology Program.

Goodrich, Ronald. "Pedestrian Behavior: The Organization of Co-active Behavior in Public Places." A paper read at the fourth National

Seminar on the Planning, Design, and Implementation of Bicycle and Pedestrian Facilities. New Orleans. December 1975.

Harris, Marvin. *The Nature of Cultural Things*. New York: Random House, 1964.

Howard, Eliot. *Territory in Bird Life*. New York: Reprinted Atheneum Books, 1964.

Jacobs, Jane. *The Death and Life of Great American Cities*. New York: Vintage Books, 1961.

Jones, Stanley. "Non-Verbal Communication in the Streets; A Comparative Proxemics, and Analysis of Dyadic Interaction in Selected Sub-cultures of New York City." Speech given at Speech Association of America Annual Meeting. December 1969.

Kendon, Adam. "Movement Coordination in Social Interaction," *Acta Psychologica* 32, 1970, pp. 100–25.

Kendon, A., and Ferber, A. "A Description of Some Behavior Greetings" in Michael, R. P. and Cook, J. H. (eds.), *Comparative Ecology and the Behaviour of Primates*. London: Academic Press, 1973.

Lattimore, Owen. *Inner Asian Frontiers of China*. Boston: Beacon Press, 1940.

Liebow, Elliot. *Tally's Corner*. Boston: Little, Brown and Co., 1967.

Lorenz, Konrad. *King Solomon's Ring*. New York: Crowell, 1952.

Lorenz, Konrad. *On Aggression*. New York: Harcourt, 1966.

Newman, Oscar. *Defensible Space: Crime Prevention Through Urban Design*. New York: Macmillan Co., 1972.

Porterfield, A. L. *Cultures of Violence*. Fort Worth, Texas: Potishman Foundation, 1965.

Scheflen, A. E. *Body Language and Social Order: Communication as Behavioral Control*. Englewood Cliffs, N.J.: Prentice-Hall, 1972.

Scheflen, A. E., with Ashcraft, N. *Human Territories*. Englewood Cliffs, N.J.: Prentice-Hall, 1975.

Sjoberg, Gideon. *The Pre-Industrial City: Past and Present*. New York: The Free Press, 1960.

Sklar, J., and Berkov, B. "The American Birth Rate: Evidences of a Coming Rise," *Science*, V. 189, N. 4204, Aug. 1975, pp. 693–700.

Sommer, R. *Personal Space* Englewood Cliffs, N.J.: Prentice-Hall, 1969.

Thacker, C. M. "Ethnic Change in the Urban Sub-area: A Study of the Dynamics of Residential Mobility." Unpublished Doctoral Dissertation, 1973. Fordham University.

Valentine, Charles. *Culture and Poverty*. Chicago: University of Chicago Press, 1968.

Vine, I. *Social Spacing in Animals and Man*. In press.

Watson, J. B. *Behaviorism*. New York: Norton, 1924.

INDEX